Embracing the Earth

Embracing the Earth

by d. mark harris

choices for environmentally sound living

Cover design and illustrations by Lyn Pusztai

THE NOBLE PRESS

Printed in the United States of America

Library of Congress Cataloging-in-Publication Data

Harris, D. Mark 1960-

   Embracing the earth: choices for environmentally sound living/

by D. Mark Harris; illustrations by Lyn Pusztai.

      p.   cm.

   ISBN 0-9622683-2-1: $9.95

      1. Environmental protection--Citizen participation. I. Pusztai,

Lyn, 1960-   . II. Title.

TD171.7.H37   1990   90-60018

363.7'0525--DC20   CIP

Noble Press books are available in bulk at discount prices. Single copies are available prepaid direct from the publisher. Contact:

Marketing Director

The Noble Press, Inc.
213 W. Institute Place, Suite 508
Chicago, IL 60610

Printed on recycled paper

To Tesia, who makes it all worthwhile

table of contents

part one: starting out

Chapter 1
Reduce: Keeping Valuable Resources Out of the Trash   **1**

Buy products with minimal packaging; Unwrap over-packaged goods in the store; Buy in bulk; Protest against excess packaging; Buy products built to last; Rent or borrow items you use infrequently; Repair and mend damaged items; Stop receiving junk mail; Use both sides of the paper when photocopying; Use a live Christmas tree

Chapter 2
Reuse: Once Is Not Enough   **7**

Use refillable containers; Reuse plastic wrap and aluminum foil; Use cloth instead of paper; Use mugs and glasses instead of styrofoam and paper cups; Use a lunch box instead of a bag; Use rechargeable batteries; Avoid disposable products; Bring your own shopping bag; Return hangers to the dry cleaners; Use cloth diapers; Shave with soap and a brush; Other things you can reuse: Bottles and jars, plastic bottles, paper, envelopes, greeting cards

Chapter 3
Recycle: Products Back Into Products   **15**

Take old items to second-hand shops; Hold a garage sale; Compost your organic wastes; Participate in recycling efforts; How to set up a recycling station in your home; What you can recycle: newspapers, aluminum, steel or tin cans, glass containers, plastic, batteries, tires, motor oil, organic wastes, refrigerants, other items; Buy recycled products; Start an office recycling program; Spread the word; For more information

Mix your own non-toxic cleaning solutions; Buy toxic-free cleansers; Handle toxic solutions with care; Dispose of household toxics properly; Use phosphate-free laundry detergents; Use natural insecticides for household pests; Eliminate indoor air pollutants; Keep your lawn toxic free; Buy organic food; Grow your own organic food; Find the toxics being released in your community; TOXNET; For more information

Wash dishes by hand instead of in a dishwasher; Fill your dishwasher before using; Don't wash dishes when the water's running; Turn off water when brushing your teeth, washing your face, and shaving; Install faucet aerators; Repair leaky faucets; Take a shower instead of a bath; Install a low-flow showerhead; Put a water displacer in your toilet tank; Install a low-flush toilet; Install a composting toilet; Don't leave the water running when washing your car; Sweep instead of hose off driveways and sidewalks; Water plants and lawns in the evening; Buy plants native to the area; Get more information

Audit your home's energy use; Insulation: Caulk and weatherstrip windows and doors; Install storm windows or low-emissivity windows; Insulate; Close off unused rooms; Close off your fireplace; Heating: Clean off registers and vents; Turn down the thermostat; Use space heaters; Wear warm clothing; Use a humidifier; Turn the heat way down when you go to bed; Get the most out of your furnace; Cooling: Plant trees; Keep heat out of the house; Install kitchen and bathroom fans; Use window units when possible; Raise thermostats in central air systems; Locate thermostats away from heating sources; Keep registers and vents clear; Use a dehumidifier; Install a vent fan in the attic; Get the most out of your central air system; Laundry: *Do full loads; Presoak dirty laundry; Wash with cold or warm water when possible; Don't use too much detergent; Use a James hand washing machine; Dry clothes on a clothesline; Fill clothes dryers; Dry heavy and light clothing separately; Use automatic dry cycle; Keep lint screen clean; Hang clothes to be ironed in the shower;* Lighting: *Turn off lights when you don't need them; Dust off light bulbs and lamp shades; Use low wattage light bulbs whenever possible; Use lamps with three-way switches and dimmers; Use photoelectric cells or timers; Use fluorescent lighting; Buy compact fluorescent or halogen light bulbs; Where to get compact fluorescent and halogen lamps; Install automatic flood lights; Use solar powered outdoor lights; Decorate with light colors;* In the Kitchen: *Use manual instead of electrical appliances; Check an appliance's energy rating before you buy it; Boil liquids in a lidded pot; Heat pots on the right-sized burner; Turn off electric burners or ovens before a job is done; Use small appliances for small jobs; Use the oven for multiple jobs; Don't open the oven door; Make a solar box cooker; Do small dish loads by hand; Fill up your dishwasher; Don't use the dishwasher's drying cycle; Scrape your dishes; Don't put hot food in the refrigerator right away; Regulate your refrigerator's temperature; Don't open up fridge and freezer doors frequently; Keep your fridge well maintained; Buy a Sunfrost refrigerator/freezer;* Hot Water: *Use cold water whenever possible; Cut back on hot water use; Service your hot water tank; Work with your local utility; For more information*

part two: getting more involved

Don't buy products made from endangered or threatened animals; Report poaching; Adopt an animal: Whale Adoption Project, Project Wind Seine; Delaware Valley Raptor Center, Adopt-A-Deer, Adopt-A-Horse Program; Volunteer at animal protection groups; Boycott tuna fish; Cut up six-pack rings; Build a backyard wildlife habitat

Plant a tree; How to plant a tree; Join a tree planting organization; Tree-planting organizations; Spread the word with seed greeting cards; Get more information

Keep abreast of what's happening in your neighborhood; Write to your congressperson; How to write a letter to your congressperson; Call your congressperson; Follow the voting record of your congressperson; Vote; Protest; Boycott environmentally unsound products and manufacturers; BUYcott; Support the Valdez Principles

Get more involved; How to choose an organization to support

part three: going all the way

State of the World; Influential environmental books; Environmental magazines; The Legislative Hotline; EcoNet; Environmental television programs; Environmental films and videos

part four: the directories

introduction

The 1990s will, I think, be a time when we finally come to the realization that our lifestyles are causing irreparable damage to the environment. This knowledge won't come as a surprise; it's something most of us have known, or at least suspected, for some time now. For years we've opened the morning newspaper and read the studies on acid rain, global warming, and rainforest destruction, and we've listened to the gloomy litany of a steady succession of environmental prophets: Aldo Leopold, David Brower, Lois Gibbs, Dave Foreman. We believed what we read and heard, but we couldn't help feeling that the seriousness of these environmental problems was somehow overblown, especially since they never confronted us on a personal level. We could read about massive oil leaks contaminating groundwater supplies, and industrial smokestacks emitting record amounts of toxic fumes, but rarely was there any evidence of it in our neighborhoods. The air outside still smelled fresh and the water out of the kitchen tap tasted as good as it always had.

The difference now is that we are coming face-to-face with the results of our irresponsibility. We can't take our children to the lakes and rivers we once fished and swam in because the waters are polluted; ozone and air pollution alerts prevent us from taking our daily jog around the park; we buy bottled water because the water out of the tap tastes funny; we're afraid to buy fresh produce from the grocery store because we can't be sure that it's free of pesticides. With our health and quality of life in jeopardy, we're getting angry and anxious, and are starting to wonder how things ever got to be this way. And it's in our search for answers that we are beginning to see the connection between our lifestyles and the environmental crises happening in our own backyards. We are slowly coming to recognize that when we drive to work every day in a car that gets 15 miles to the gallon we are contributing to the problem. And that the same thing happens when we leave the lights on in empty rooms, or run the air conditioning at 65 degrees, or throw recyclable newspapers and aluminum cans into the trash. I think we'll make even more of these mental connections as the decade progresses and pollution intrudes even further into our lives.

Mere recognition won't solve the problem, however. We need to take concrete steps to lessen our burden on the earth; we need to take specific actions within our lives and in our homes that will reduce the amount of valuable resources we use up, and limit the amount of pollution and waste we generate. But it's not always easy to know what to do or how to go about it, as I discovered a few years ago when I first attempted to live more responsibly. We've gotten out of the habit of saving and making do with less. Relearning how to do these things will take some effort and creativity. In my search for how to live a more environmentally sound lifestyle I came across a lot of advice, suggestions, useful products, and sources of information. In this book I pass along these resources to you in order to make your own search easier.

Embracing the Earth is essentially about thrift and responsibility--forgotten, old-fashioned virtues that used to determine the way people looked at the world and their role in it. You'll recognize bits of old, practical wisdom in the many suggestions here. And since many of them are obvious, you'll be tempted to read over them quickly. But I encourage you to examine them closely and to try to apply them to your life. I think you'll admit that, in many cases, these suggestions are more commonly heard than acted on. Sure, you know that turning off the lights in unused rooms saves energy, but do you still tend to leave them on? Broken furniture can be repaired and torn clothes can be mended, but do you ever really make the effort? Or do you throw them out and buy new ones? You know that luxury automobiles tend to get horrendously poor gas mileage, and you know that a car is not a reflection of a person's worth. But do you own one, and do you use it more than you need to? These are questions we need to start honestly asking ourselves, and this book encourages you to ask them. We need to resurrect our sense of responsibility to the earth if we are going to have any chance of solving the environmental crisis.

The book also offers the latest information on new technologies and products that can help you save resources. Energy-efficient appliances, water saving devices, and solar products are just a few that are mentioned, along with all the information you need to acquire them and to make the most of your purchase.

I have tried to make this book as practical, accessible, and complete as possible. However, I know that it is just a start, that there are more useful, insightful, and practical ways of living more responsibly. I welcome your comments, criticisms, and suggestions, and offer this book as a forum for your ideas. Best of luck in your search for a more environmentally sound, and more fulfilling, life.

acknowledgments

This book would not have taken form were it not for Lyn Pusztai. Her encouragement, support, and most of all, her art were continual sources of inspiration throughout this project. The importance of her contribution is visible on every page.

Rik Scarce, environmentalist, author, and soon to be doctoral student, was an unending source of information. His suggestions and words of wisdom can be found in each chapter. He will be repaid in full with Miller Tallboys, but let these words of thanks suffice until then. Rob Wieboldt had the unenviable job of digging up research materials in the library, and he helped me determine the book's focus. Many environmentalists and entrepreneurs gave me the benefit of their hard-won knowledge; they work every day in the trenches and have sustained the movement during the worst of times. Tesia, my wife, carefully edited and proofed the manuscript, and greatly added to it with her advice and insights. She has done a lot of the dirty work in implementing and experimenting with the "choices" in this book. Julia Bogardus read and proofed the manuscript and made invaluable suggestions for improvements and changes. I would also like to thank Lee Anne Unterbrink for her artistic direction on the cover and work on production.

And finally, thanks to my friends at the Noble Press: David Driver, Mary-Terese Cozzola, and Elaine Tite, who believed in this project.

part one

starting out

> *"Near the end of March I borrowed an axe and went down to the woods near Walden Pond. I returned it sharper than I received it."*
>
> Thoreau, *Walden*

CHAPTER 1

REDUCE
KEEPING VALUABLE RESOURCES OUT OF THE TRASH

The clothes in your closet, the soft drink cans in the refrigerator, the car in the garage--literally all the things you buy and use--are made from valuable resources. Over 500,000 trees are cut down every week to make the paper in our Sunday newspaper; the amount of materials that is used every year to make cans, foil, and other aluminum products could rebuild all the airplanes in the commercial airline industry every three months. And more often than not, once transformed into usable products these resources are then thrown away after one use, hauled to the curb in plastic bags and carted off to burgeoning landfills.

But by cutting back on the products you buy or use, you reduce the demand for them and, eventually, the amount of resources that are used up to make them. When the demand for paper shrinks because you refuse to buy products in excess packaging or because your office starts photocopying on both sides of the paper, fewer trees will be chopped down. And in the process you'll cut down on the amount of trash you have to throw away or recycle (remember, recycling uses up energy and resources too). Our wealth is in our resources; we need to use them wisely.

Buy products with minimal packaging

Avoid buying products needlessly entombed in packaging. Aspirin bottles don't need to be put in a box, fruits and vegetables don't have to be covered in styrofoam and plastic, each slice of cheese doesn't need to be individually wrapped; there's no reason for "beauty aids" and health products to be put in boxes. If a similar product that is responsibly packaged is available, buy it instead of the overpackaged one.

Unwrap over-packaged goods in the store

Let's face it--some of the things you need to buy will be wrapped in enough packaging to cover a product three times its size. But you can still keep the packaging out of your trash can by removing the product from its box, plastic wrapping, or styrofoam container right there in the store and leaving the packaging on the shelf. Take broccoli off its plastic-covered styrofoam plate, remove the jar of facial cream from its box, take the bag off the head of lettuce, and leave the wrappings on the shelf. If enough people do this, the store manager will get the message. Better yet, tell the manager of your disgust with excess packaging and of your plans to leave it on the shelf. Encourage her to stop carrying over-packaged goods.

Be aware, however, that you will not make friends with the checkout tellers, since the price stickers and bar codes they need to ring up your bill are on the packaging. This is the first line of resistance, but don't be scared off. If enough irritated tellers complain to their bosses about constantly having to break their routine to check prices, store managers will be forced to confront the problem of over-packaging. If you're uncomfortable with this, remember the price of the product and tell it to the teller when you reach the checkout line. A lot of them would rather believe you than wait for a bagger to go check it.

Buy in bulk

A lot of non-perishable foods can be bought in bulk. Pastas, rice, dried fruits, grains, nuts, candies, and bagels come most readily to mind; open bins of candy, flour, and even grated cheese are available in some places. Food bought in bulk is almost always cheaper, and packaging is left to a minimum. And since you won't have to go to the grocery store as often to stock up, you'll save time and transportation costs. Look for the bulk barrels in your grocery store. (If your grocery store doesn't have bulk barrels, tell the manager you want them. Have your friends follow up with similar requests). And don't forget to bring a bag or container to hold your fill. Most bulk food areas have plastic bags, but you're not really reducing packaging unless you bring your own reusable container. When you get home, store your dry goods in old glass jars--mayonnaise and pickle jars are especially good.

If certain foodstuffs are not available in bulk bins, then buy them in the largest-sized package. Buy bagels that come 12 to a pack instead of 4, or 10-pound bags of flour instead of 5-pound bags. Far less packaging is used to make one 10-pound bag than two 5-pound ones.

Protest against excess packaging

Your attempts to reduce packaging will be more effective if you follow them up with letters of complaint to the food manufacturers. Tell them you will continue to buy their competitors' products until they reduce their packaging. Let the manager of your local grocery store know of your actions and encourage her to join in your boycott. The company's address can usually be found somewhere on the packaging; send your letters to the company's Consumer Affairs Division.

Buy products built to last

Poorly made products are quickly worn out and thrown away. When buying something you need, make sure it's designed to handle the work it was made for and that it will hold up to repeated performance. This doesn't just pertain to mechanical objects; it includes clothes, tools, books, furniture–literally everything you use. Quality products usually cost more, but they are almost always worth it. To find out which products are best, look in back issues of *Consumer Reports*, or in its annual buying guide, which rates a variety of products from automobiles to hair dryers.

Rent or borrow items you use infrequently

Energy and valuable resources went into making that product you used only once and stored in the garage. If you need to use an item only one time or on a short-term basis, borrow it from a friend or rent it from a renting and leasing company. Rental companies offer everything from lawn furniture, builder's tools, and ladders, to crutches, beds, and china. And who knows what sort of seldom-used treasures your friends have. Also consider buying things as a community, such as a wheelbarrow or a washer and dryer. Ten neighbors chip in to pay for one washer, when they otherwise would have bought 10 of them individually. It saves you a lot of money and it saves the earth's resources.

Repair and mend damaged items

How many times have you thrown away something you've torn or broken, which, with a little effort, could have been repaired? Socks with holes in them can be darned, ripped and broken furniture can be reupholstered or reglued. If you can't or don't want to fix something, take it to someone who can. Most dry cleaners will mend and alter your clothes (ours keeps sewing up my backpack), furniture makers will fix broken chairs, jewelers will repair broken watches. When something is broken, think first about how to salvage and fix it instead of throwing it away and buying a replacement.

Stop receiving junk mail

Every year we receive over 2 million tons of junk mail, almost half of which we never even open. Opened or not, it all eventually is thrown away. To stem the flow of junk mail that invades your mailbox and fills up your garbage can, write to the Direct Marketing Association and ask them to take your name off their mailing list. DMA will stop selling your name to companies using large mailing lists. This will only affect companies that don't already have your name; to get off an existing list, write to the company sending you the junk mail. Contact: Direct Marketing Association, 6 East 43rd St., New York, NY 10017.

You can also stuff prepaid return envelopes with the junk mail sent to you (including the envelope!). Enclose a note asking the sender to take you off his list, and send it all back to him. He pays for getting his junk mail back, and you free yourself from the company's garbage at the company's cost. A friend of mine, who is really upset about junk mail, wraps a brick with his junk mail and pastes the prepaid return envelope to it. The sender of the junk mail pays for the cost of receiving a brick.

Use both sides of the paper when photocopying

This takes a little effort and some planning, especially for big jobs, but you'll cut in half the amount of paper you use. To be even more environmentally conscious, use copying paper made from recycled paper. See the service directory for recycled paper companies that offer Simpson paper, a brand specially manufactured for copying machines.

Use a live, potted tree for a Christmas tree

Thirty-four million Christmas trees are chopped down every year, each only to last a few weeks before being hauled away to overburdened landfills. Instead of encouraging this waste of natural resources and abetting the landfill problem, buy a live tree. The tree can be decorated year after year, and be repotted as it grows. If you want to plant the tree in your yard after the holidays, get a tree that is indigenous to your area. Native trees are easier to transplant, need less water, and become healthier plants. For more information, contact your local nursery or write The National Arbor Day Foundation, 100 Arbor Avenue, Nebraska City, NE 68410.

If you still want to buy that temporary tree, be sure to have it mulched when you're through with it. Many municipalities offer the service free of charge, and either let you keep the mulch, or use it themselves in city parks and landscaping.

"There must be a limit to how much cloth you can cram into any one house, but of course it's disposable. You used to buy for quality, things that would last. You kept your clothes until they were part of you."

Margaret Atwood, *Cat's Eye*

CHAPTER 2

REUSE
ONCE IS NOT ENOUGH

One morning while shaving, King C. Gillette was struck by an idea that would forever change the way men shaved--a razor with replaceable blades. The year was 1895; almost a hundred years later, Americans are throwing away 2 billion razor blades a year. Seeing diaper washing for the messy job it is, Procter & Gamble in 1961 introduced a diaper that could be tossed out after one use. The new product sold like hotcakes, and nearly thirty years later Americans are discarding over 18 billion disposable diapers every year.

The stories are different but the ending is the same: a reusable product was replaced by a disposable one. And how quickly we caught on, throwing away 1.6 billion pens a year, 45 billion paper cups, 25 billion styrofoam containers, 348 million lighters, and untold numbers of cameras, phones and travel irons (yes, travel irons), all designed to be chucked out after a few uses. We've enjoyed the convenience, but we are quickly discovering that disposable products come with a cost. The problem with making disposable products is that it assumes (1) there is an unending supply of raw materials to make new ones, and (2) there is a place to throw the old ones away. Burgeoning landfills and the destruction of valuable resources--to say nothing of pollution--are finally showing us the limits of this arrogant way of thinking. It's time we went back to an old idea that works well: only buy something you can use over and over again.

Use refillable containers

Instead of wrapping your leftovers in plastic that's headed for the waste can after it has been used, store them in reusable containers. Tupperware and Rubbermaid plastic containers are airtight, come in a variety of sizes, can be put in microwaves and freezers, and can be used over and over again. Use them to keep leftovers fresh, to freeze your homemade spaghetti sauce, and to store your dry goods.

Reuse plastic wrap and aluminum foil

We have been encouraged to believe that plastic wrap, aluminum foil, and other storage materials can only be used once, when in fact they can be reused many times over. We wash our plastic wrap and foil after each use and let them dry overnight. The plastic retains its cling and the foil is just as pliable as a new piece. Instead of buying new wrap every few weeks, you'll find you need to buy it only once a year.

Use cloth instead of paper

Paper napkins, towels, and tissues have reusable counterparts in cloth. And because of its reusability, cloth is cheaper and, in most cases, even better at its job than paper. We have a couple of sets of cloth napkins and dishtowels--as well as a bag full of rags--which we change about once a week and throw in with our laundry. Use your old clothing for rags. Discarded socks, tee shirts, and even underwear make it into our bag of rags, and we use them for dusting, wiping up spills, washing the car, and many house-cleaning chores.

Use mugs and glasses instead of styrofoam and paper cups

This one is simple: glasses and mugs are quickly washed out and reused; styrofoam and paper cups are tossed out after one use and added to landfills. Styrofoam cups are especially bad, since they are made from compounds which destroy the ozone layer. Bring a glass or mug to work. If you get your morning cup of coffee at the same place every day, get a reusable plastic mug (with a lid) and have the server fill it up. Some places even give you discounts on coffee if you buy their mugs and bring them in for refills. I carry a plastic mug in my backpack and pull it out when I buy coffee, especially when only styrofoam cups are offered.

Use a lunch box instead of a bag

Lunch boxes have traditionally been used by school kids and construction workers; more of us should follow their lead. Lunch boxes are reusable and will last for years, to say nothing of their ability to keep your peanut butter and jelly sandwich from becoming a breaded wad. Check out the new offering of attractive lunch boxes--they have come a long way since you were in grade school.

Use rechargeable batteries

Rechargeable nickel-cadmium batteries cost about three times the amount of regular batteries, but they can be recharged and reused up to a hundred times. General Electric's Ni-Cads are probably the easiest to find. If you're uneasy about supporting GE (it makes more components for nuclear weapons than any other company), contact SunWatt, a solar energy company out of Maine, which puts out a good line of heavy duty Ni-Cad rechargeable batteries.

With all rechargeable batteries, you'll need to get a charger, which plugs into a standard electrical socket. Chargers can run you anywhere from $10 to $50, depending on the brand and the number of batteries it can hold. Eveready and General Electric both make chargers; Sun-Watt makes a line of inexpensive solar battery chargers, which can even rejuvenate ordinary dry-cell batteries a limited number of times. See SunWatt in the service directory.

Avoid disposable products

Many types of flashlights, cigarette lighters, razors, writing pens, and even cameras are made to be thrown away after a few uses. Don't buy them. Buy pens that have replaceable cartridges, lighters that can be refilled, flashlights that can be rejuvenated with new batteries (make sure you use rechargeable batteries). You'll save money, shopping time, and trips to the garbage can.

Bring your own shopping bag

Bringing your own bag or bags to the grocery store may confuse the baggers–one bagger recently placed a paper bag inside my reusable string one--but it will save you from collecting unwanted stacks of paper and plastic bags. I bring my college-style backpack with me whenever I go to the store. It can hold a lot of stuff and the padded shoulder straps make carrying even heavy loads pretty easy. I keep a large string bag in one of the sidepockets for the purchases that don't fit into the pack.

The Europeans have long used reusable string bags to carry their groceries home. They fit into your pocket, are good for countless trips to the store, and hold as much as a regular grocery bag. You can find them here in the States at some gourmet grocery stores. Seventh Generation also sells them through the mail for $8.95 a pair. See Seventh Generation in the service directory. You can also use old shopping bags to carry your groceries home. Put them away after you've used them and bring them with you when you go shopping again.

Return hangers to the dry cleaners

If you're like many people who use dry cleaners frequently, you have a closet full of empty hangers you'll never use. Take them back to a place that has a use for them--the dry cleaners. When you pick up your clothes, remove the plastic wrapper draped over your clothes and ask the server to reuse it. Each time you go, ask the server not to give you plastic (make sure he writes this down on the bill!). If you absolutely need the plastic over your clothes to keep them from getting dirty or wet on the way home, take the plastic off later and return it to the dry cleaners on your next visit.

Use cloth diapers

Every year, we throw away 18 billion disposable diapers, which required 250,000 trees and 82,000 tons of plastic to be manufactured. And once discarded, they are added to dwindling landfill space, where diseases in fecal matter can leach into and contaminate groundwater supplies. Disposable diapers may be easy, but they have huge environmental consequences. Cloth diapers, on the other hand, can be used and reused. And when they've finally outlasted their usefulness they can be made into rags. They're cheaper, too. One study found that the cost of using cloth diapers was about $10 a month, as compared to $80 a month for disposables.

Buying cloth diapers

Most children go through a dozen diapers a day. Cloth diapers usually come in boxes of twelve, so figure out how often you want to do laundry, and buy accordingly. A box of twelve will cost you about $10. With cloth diapers, you'll need diaper covers. Avoid plastic. There are good natural fiber covers on the market from $10 on.

Diaper services

Although twice as expensive as doing the diapers yourself, a diaper service can save you a lot of time and effort. For a weekly fee of anywhere from $15 to $20 per child, a service will supply you with about 90 cloth diapers, which they will pick up and deliver to your home once a week. Anti-odor containers and diaper covers are extra. You don't even have to scoop the poop out; services flush the excrement into sewer treatment plants before washing, leaving groundwater supplies uncontaminated. My neighbors swear by their service. For them the biggest advantage is having a stack of diapers on hand for any use, not just as diapers. They use them as burping cloths, hand towels to wipe off their babies' dirty hands and faces, and rags to clean up spills. The diapers are so absorbent that the husband uses them to dry off his car. When they are finished with the "diaper rags," they pop them in the container and the service washes all of them. To locate the diaper service in your area, look under "Diaper Service" in the Yellow Pages. You can also contact the National Association of Diaper Services, 2017 Walnut St., Philadelphia, PA 19103; 215-569-3650, for a list of services in your area.

The Biodegradable Diaper: A Non-Solution

In response to consumer concerns about the garbage crisis, a number of diaper manufacturers have produced a "biodegradable" diaper. In these diapers the plastic covering is made from a cornstarch resin, which decomposes in a landfill in about two years. However, these biodegradable diapers still do not address the problems posed by regular disposable diapers--they consume just as much wood pulp and plastic, which still end up in over-burdened landfills, and the fecal matter retained in them may still contaminate groundwater supplies. The environmental impact of degraded cornstarch is also not fully understood. Furthermore, it is unclear whether so-called "biodegradable" diapers ever really decompose in landfills where they receive little or none of the light and air necessary for decomposition.

For further information

Mothering, an enlightened magazine on parenting, is a good source on diaper services and products. Subscriptions are $18/year for 4 issues. Contact Mothering, P.O. Box 1690, Sante Fe, NM 87504.

Shave with soap and a brush

Gillette, Johnson and Co., and Barbasol have tried hard over the years to convince us that shaving cream comes only from a disposable can. But for decades men have given themselves perfectly good, close shaves using a plain bar of soap and a reusable mug and brush. Drop a bar of soap into a mug, cover it with hot water, and stir the soap with the brush to create a hot lather. There is no can to throw away, and the lather doesn't contain the ammonia and ethanol often present in can creams. You can usually find barbershop style mugs and brushes at department stores and cutlery shops; Hoffritz and Franklin Toiletry both sell a shaving kit that comes with a mug, brush and stand, soap bar, and razor. Also look in antique stores.

Other things you can reuse

Bottles and jars. Old juice bottles, and jars that held jelly, pickles, peanut butter, coffee, peanuts, mayonnaise and anything else, can have a useful second life. We use our large bottles to brew sun tea and to hold our morning orange juice. Jars are turned into short-term transplanting pots and penny jars, or used as containers for tea and coffee, rice, oatmeal, and dried mushrooms. Glass containers come with good tops, so they are airtight and keep your dry goods fresh.

Plastic bottles. If you want to buy glass bottles because of their recyclability but have a hard time giving up the convenience and safety of plastic, buy glass bottles and transfer the contents to used plastic bottles. It's tough to beat the convenience of the squeezable ketchup bottle, so we get ketchup in glass bottles and pour it into our one squeezable bottle.

Paper. Take a stack of used paper and make a notepad out of it. Write on the backside of the paper.

Envelopes, especially the large, brown, business kind. Open the ones you receive with care and reuse them. Cover over the old address with tape or an address label. Old stamps and metered postage stickers can be peeled off, and new postage added.

Greeting cards. Cut the pictures out of greeting cards and use them for labels on gifts. Or put them in with the rest of your art supplies and let your children use them for art projects.

CHAPTER 3

RECYCLE

PRODUCTS BACK INTO PRODUCTS

Our current garbage crisis is really the result of linear thinking. Resources are converted into products, which we use a few times and throw away. There is a line straight from the place where we cut down the tree or mine the earth to the garbage heap. Recycling, on the other hand, is as its name suggests, circular, taking that used product and turning it back into something that can be used again. Recycled cans are made into new cans, newspaper is made into cardboard, plastic bottles become park benches. The "trash" is converted into a new product, and if done right, it never reaches the garbage pile at all.

Recycling is a concept that we Americans have been slow to catch on to. We comprise less than a tenth of the world's population but generate more trash than any other country--some 1,500 pounds per person every year. Only 10% of it is ever recycled. West Germany generates less than half the amount of trash we do, and recycles 30% of it. Japan, our biggest economic competitor, has also badly beaten us on the recycling front. It recycles over 50% of its trash, half of all its wastepaper and glass bottles, more than 60% of its drink and food cans. These countries have been quick to realize that recycling not only reduces wastes and preserves resources, but it also brings in money, creates jobs, and cuts down on energy needs and pollution. Recycling is an idea whose time has long since come, and we need to adopt it if we are going to have any hope of solving the garbage crisis in this country.

Take old items to secondhand shops

Goodwill Industries, the Salvation Army, churches, and hospitals are among the many organizations that recycle goods through secondhand shops. They accept almost anything, including clothes, furniture, books, tools, and dishware, and fix them up for resale. The next time you need to buy something and don't need it to be brand new, look for it in a secondhand shop. My wife and I have bought perfectly good bicycles, books, suits, and even greeting cards at our local white elephant store. Our money went to support a good cause--Goodwill Industries--and we can write off on our taxes the value of the things we have donated there.

Hold a garage sale

If you have so much stuff to get rid of that you'd have to take four or five trips down to Goodwill, hold a garage sale. When a neighbor buys an item of yours that you always thought was particularly hideous, you'll see that one man's junk is truly another man's treasure. Encourage others to recycle their "junk," and hold a neighborhood garage sale.

Compost your organic wastes

The basic idea behind composting is to put all your organic wastes--everything from yard clippings to kitchen scraps --into a big pile and let them decompose. The finished compost can then be tilled into the soil or applied as mulch for plants. That's the basic idea, but there are *lots* of different theories about the best way to compost, from digging a big hole in the ground and dumping your garbage into it, to constructing high-tech hot composting bins and regularly turning the refuse. Talk to a gardening neighbor or someone at your local gardening club or horticultural center for ideas. Two books, *Rodale's Guide to Composting* and *Let It Rot! The Complete Gardener's Guide to Composting* will show you how to construct bins and maintain a good compost pile. For $2.50, the Seattle Tilth Association will send you, "Home Composting," an easy guide to composting. Send a stamped, self-addressed envelope, with 50 cents postage, to Seattle Tilth Association, 4649 Sunnyside Ave., Seattle, WA 98103.

Participate in recycling efforts

Most of the work of recycling is carried out by local recycling centers, which accept recyclable materials and sell them to reprocessing centers. You cart your newspapers and aluminum cans over to the center, which pays you a minimal sum for them. Like any business, recycling centers have their own personalities and agendas. Some are only interested in materials that make the most money --aluminum cans, newspapers, and glass--while others are out to collect as much recyclable material as they can find markets for. Call your recycling center (under "recycling" in the Yellow Pages) to find out what materials it accepts and how the center wants it brought to them. Most centers, for instance, want all cans crushed and bottles separated by color, but some may want them washed out and the paper labels removed from the cans as well. To find out the location of the recycling center nearest you, contact the Environmental Defense Fund, 257 Park Avenue South, New York, NY 10010; 212-505-2100.

Recently, a larger share of recycling has been done through community recycling programs. You'll know if your neighborhood has such a program, because you will most likely be required to participate. The program will give you all the information you need, as well as special containers to hold your separated materials. During the week, you separate your materials into the appropriate containers and take them to the corner on pickup day as you would with a regular trash service. Call your city hall for more information. If your city doesn't have a recycling program, start one! Call your city officials. You can get technical assistance from the Institute for Local Self-Reliance, 2425 18th St., NW, Washington, DC 20009; 202-232-4108.

HOW TO SET UP A RECYCLING STATION IN YOUR HOME

Recycling will become easier and more habitual once you've set aside some corner of your house to serve as the recycling station. The kitchen is probably the best place to use--especially the area under the sink--since most of your recyclable trash will be generated there. But I've also known people to use seldom-used entryways, back porches, hall closets and garages, with equal success. Whatever spot you choose, make sure you have enough room for the amount of recyclable trash you will accumulate (which will vary depending on the amount of trash you go through and the frequency of your trips to the recycling center), as well as containers to hold it. Set aside room for:

A can for non-recyclable trash. This will hold materials that can't be recycled, such as certain kinds of plastic, wax containers for milk and juice, and non-reusable paper. Avoid using plastic bags; use a brown paper bag instead, lining the bottom with a piece of your plastic or wax garbage.

A box for glass. A box will keep your glass from rolling around, and will make transporting it to the recycling center easier. Depending on the amount of room you have, you can set up three different boxes, one each for clear, brown, and green glass (the way most centers require it to be separated). We store all our glass in one box and separate it into reusable bags before going to the recycling center.

A container for aluminum cans. A free-standing brown paper bag will do, but if you go through a lot of cans, use a large box or trash can. Crush the cans before you store them to cut down on the number of containers you have to cart to the recycling center.

A bag for metals. Use a brown bag to store various kinds of recyclable metal--cans for soup, vegetables, and fruits; bottle tops, aluminum foil, pie plates, frozen food trays, and pieces of scrap copper.

A can for organic wastes. A small can, an old pot, or a used coffee pot make good containers for kitchen scraps. Make sure it has a top to keep the bugs out. You can throw all kinds of organic wastes into it, such as coffee grounds, eggshells, and tea bags, which can be added to your compost pile.

A bag for plastic. More and more places are accepting plastic for recycling. This includes milk jugs, soft drink bottles, and plastic bags. Check which plastic materials your recycling center accepts and make room for the appropriate size bag.

Bags for newspapers. Grocery bags are perfect for newspapers. As you fill them, stack them on top of one another to save space. You can also tie together stacks of papers with string.

WHAT YOU CAN RECYCLE AND HOW TO PREPARE IT

Newspapers

First, remove any glossy paper and magazine inserts from your newspapers. Colored paper, such as the comics section, is O.K. for recycling, but don't mix in other types of paper that aren't strictly newsprint. Then load your newspapers into grocery bags or bind them into stacks with string. Newspapers are recycled to make more newspapers, as well as cereal boxes, construction paper, and home insulation.

Aluminum

This does not just include aluminum cans. Aluminum foil, trays from frozen foods, pie plates, old lawn furniture, and even gutters and house siding can be recycled. Rinse the aluminum and remove any paper labels. Flattening the cans will save room in your recycling bag. (Seventh Generation sells an easy-to-use can crusher for $25). Some grocery stores have machines that accept cans individually and pay you for them. Most recycled aluminum goes back into making new cans.

A note of warning: Some beverage companies have begun packaging drinks in bi-metal cans, containers with metal bodies and aluminum tops. Although they can be recycled, bi-metal cans must first be separated from their all-aluminum counterparts and then processed separately. These extra steps are costly (extra people and machinery are needed), and are a needless drain on successful recycling efforts. Avoid buying these cans; you can determine if a can is bi-metal by putting a magnet to the body. If it adheres, the can is bi-metal. These cans also lack the "Recyclable Aluminum" logo that appears on all-aluminum containers.

Steel or tin cans

Most of the cans for soup and fruits and vegetables are made out of steel. Rinse them out and remove the paper labels.

Glass containers

Glass usually needs to be separated by color: clear, green, and brown/amber. Rinse and remove lids, corks, outer linings, and rings. (Some bottle caps can be recycled with scrap metals; make sure to remove any plastic lining inside the cap). Don't worry about paper labels; they are removed during the recycling process. Recycling centers accept glass that is broken or cracked, since glass is ground down during the recycling process. Don't mix glass from window panes or light bulbs in with your other glass products. The glass in these products is manufactured in a different way and can't be combined with other glass.

Plastic

More and more recycling programs are accepting plastic, primarily soft drinks bottles (PET–polyethylene tereph-thalate) and milk jugs (HDPE–high density polyethylene); some also take detergent bottles and plastic garbage and grocery bags. Rinse and remove plastic and metal caps from bottles. Call first to see if your program accepts squeezable bottles. They are made from a combination of plastics and are difficult to recycle. Recycled plastic is used to make park benches, street signs, carpeting, and tire stoppers in parking spaces.

Batteries

A few recycling programs accept household batteries for recycling. They extract mercury and other metals from them (jewelers have been removing the silver from them for years), and dispose of the remainder of the battery in toxic disposal sites. The technology in this area is in its infancy. Car batteries are recycled for their lead. Call your recycling center or local garage for more information.

Tires

Some recycling centers take used tires and send them off to be reprocessed as carpet backing, shingles, buckets, gaskets, and even asphalt additive. One company in California burns the tires to fuel a power plant. But call your recycling center before you bring in your used tires. Tire recycling is just gearing up, and not many centers are equipped to handle it. If your center doesn't take them, check out your local gas station or scrap yard. But make sure the tires you give them end up in recycling efforts and not in landfills. If none of these places will accept your tires, contact the Tire Retread Information Bureau, P.O. Box 811, Pebble Beach, CA 93953; 408-649-0944 or National Tire Dealers and Retreaders, 1343 L Street, NW, Washington, DC 20005; 202-789-2300.

Motor oil

Some gas stations, oil change shops, and recycling centers will take your used motor oil, but they will charge you a couple of bucks to do it. They send it off to refiners who recycle it to make lubricating oil and ship fuel.

Organic wastes

If you don't have a compost pile in your yard, you might still be able to get rid of your organic wastes at your local composting facility. Composting projects are springing up all over the country, usually in conjunction with leaf and grass collection efforts. Call your local park district for information. If you don't have any luck, ask your gardening friends if they would mind if you added your organic wastes to their compost piles. We save our kitchen scraps and take them out to my sister-in-law's place, which has a compost pile in the back yard.

Refrigerants

It's not in place as of this printing, but by the end of 1990 many service stations and auto repair shops will be equipped with machines that recycle automobile air conditioner refrigerants. The recycling process will remove excess water and oil from the refrigerant and put it back into the air conditioner. Keep your eyes on your local gas station.

Other items

Among the less obvious items that some recycling centers accept are: writing paper, corrugated cardboard, brown paper bags, scrap metals (copper and brass), automobile exhaust systems, styrofoam packaging, magazines, phone books, catalogues, scrap wood, Christmas trees, furniture and appliances. Call your local program to find out what it accepts and how it wants the items brought in.

Buy recycled products

Recycling doesn't do any good unless you buy the recycled product, a concept known as "completing the loop." Start with the daily newspaper. The *Miami Herald*, the *Los Angeles Times*, and the *Chicago Sun Times* are a few of the daily papers that are printed on recycled paper. If you live in a large city and have an option between a paper made from virgin or recycled paper, buy recycled. This is also true for countless paper products. Computer paper, writing paper, greeting cards, stationery, and even toilet paper are made from recycled paper. And don't forget recycled paper in packaging. Look for the recycling logo on the package. If you're not sure if recycled paper has been used, look at the inside of the packaging; recycled paperboard is gray or tan. Kelloggs cereals, Duncan Hines cake and cookie mixes, San Giorgio Pastas, and Arm and Hammer detergent are a few of the many products that come in packaging made from recycled materials. For a listing of the major suppliers of recycled paper products see the service directory under "recycled paper".

Start an office recycling program

You can look around the office and see what needs to be done: mugs and glasses need to replace styrofoam and paper cups, cloth towels need to replace paper ones, aluminum cans need to be collected, and a lot of paper needs to be recycled. It's a big job, and it may look impossible if you work in a large office. But it can be done (The University of Chicago has instituted a successful campus-wide paper recycling program), and there are guides out there to help you . San Francisco's Recycling Program has written "Your Office Paper Recycling Guide," a step-by-step plan for turning your used office paper into recycled paper. The booklet shows you how to assess the amount of paper you're using, how to find a waste paper dealer, and how to get your fellow employees to participate. The booklet also comes with a tip sheet on how to reduce office waste. Send $12 to San Francisco Recycling Program, City Hall, Room 271, San Francisco, CA 94102; 415-554-6197. The American Paper Institute can also give you a hand. Contact American Paper Institute, 260 Madison Ave., New York, NY 10016; 212-340-0650.

Spread the word

Many people don't recycle simply because they are not aware of the recycling efforts in their area. Talk to your friends, your neighbors, your family members and encourage them to recycle. Tell them how to go about setting up a recycling station and where to go to turn in their materials. We have converted a lot of people to recycling by sharing this information.

For more information

The Environmental Defense Fund publishes "If You're Not Recycling You're Throwing It All Away," a free pamphlet that serves as a good primer to recycling. EDF also publishes *Coming Full Circle*, a useful guidebook to community recycling programs across the country. It includes case studies, a marketing analysis, a list of contact sources, and references. The cost is $20, $10 for EDF members. Contact: EDF, 257 Park Avenue South, New York, NY 10010; 212-505-2100.

"We must recognize that the best way to deal with pollution is not to let it happen in the first place. Only in this way will we be able to meet the challenge that we all live in everyone's backyard."

Lois Gibbs

CHAPTER 4

ELIMINATING TOXICS
BREATHING FREE AND LIVING HEALTHY

With all the chemical fertilizers, pesticides, fungicides, insecticides, and cleansers we use as a matter of course in our lives today, it's hard to believe that before World War II people got along perfectly well without them. Smaller, multi-crop farms used more natural agricultural methods that didn't rely on pesticides; cleaning solutions were chemical free, consisting of a little baking soda, borax, and elbow grease. But the war changed all that. Advances in chemical warfare resulted in the production of new compounds that could easily kill insects and weeds, and which, when applied to agriculture back home, would take some of the drudgery out of farm work and produce bigger, healthier crops. Watered down and packaged differently, some of these chemicals were applied to kitchen cleaning, their acids used to dissolve in seconds the dirt which rubbing took minutes to remove.

At first, the chemicals worked. They were fast and easy, and produced bumper crops. We abandoned the traditional farming methods, and in the house threw away sweat-of-the-brow cleaning powders. But the problem with pesticides is that as time went on, more of them were needed to do the same job, and when a chemical was used to kill one type of insect, another kind replaced it. We used more and more pesticides to kill more and more insects. After a while it became apparent that the chemicals were not only ineffective in increasing crop yields, but that they actually decreased crop yields, over 50% since 1945. There were even greater consequences for the environment. Runoff from pesticide-laden landscapes flowed into rivers and streams, poisoning fish and wildlife and tincturing our own drinking water supplies. While pesticides poisoned our water, cleaning solutions poisoned our homes with their toxic compounds. We spilled harmful solutions onto our skin, inhaled carcinogenic vapors into our lungs. And when we were finished with them, we poured them down the drain, releasing them untreated into waterways and delicate ecosystems.

Over a million people are poisoned by pesticides every year; of those up to 10,000 die. The number of people harmed by cleaning solutions is not as well documented, but may be just as high. And all this to do a little less work. People living in the age before the advent of pesticides and toxic cleaning solutions not only got along without them, they got along better. We need to look back and adopt methods that do less damage to ourselves and to our environment.

Mix your own non-toxic cleaning solutions

Before the appearance of commercial cleansers in the 1940s, most cleaning was done with a hard brush and a bar of soap. This method had worked fine for centuries, but manufacturers soon convinced us that to be clean, we needed to get rid of the slight film that soap leaves and to kill disease-causing germs. We've been hooked on all sorts of elaborate cleansers ever since, scrubbing our homes while toxic ingredients harm our skin, irritate our eyes, infest our lungs, and contaminate our water supply. We need to return to simple, non-toxic cleaners; they're easy to mix, they do the job, and they don't abuse the environment.

Basic ingredients

Most of your cleaning can be done with a mixture of the following non-toxic ingredients:

Soap is a salt that comes from fatty acids that are found in fats and oils. Soaps are good for cleaning, since their molecules mix well with water and cling to dirt and grease, making dirt and stains easy to wash off. Use a phosphate-free liquid soap such as Palmolive or Ivory.

Sodium bicarbonate, or baking soda as we know it, is the by-product of a very weak acid that results when carbon dioxide reacts with water. That little bit of acid gives baking soda its cleaning power. It's good for deodorizing, softening water, and scouring (since it is soft, baking soda won't abrade surfaces).

Washing soda, or sodium carbonate, is related to baking soda. It can be used to cut through grease, soften water, and disinfect.

Borax is a naturally-occurring mineral composed primarily of sodium and boron. It mixes well with water, and can be used for disinfecting, cleaning, and deodorizing.

Vinegar is a dilute acetic acid that results from the fermentation of alcohol. Household vinegar is usually further diluted to 5% acidity, giving it just enough power to cut grease. It's also good as an air freshener.

Ammonia is a gas condensed into a liquid, which is diluted with water for household use. Use it for cleaning and disinfecting, but be careful. It can inflame the respiratory tract if deeply inhaled and is toxic if mixed with other cleaning products, such as bleach or tub and tile cleaners.

Lemon juice, as taste will tell you, is acidic, a quality that enables it to cut through grease and stains. Its fragrance can also serve as an air freshener.

Recipe for an All-purpose cleaner

Hot water (1 gallon)

Borax (1/4 cup)

Vinegar (1/4 cup)

Liquid soap (2 tablespoons)

Elbow grease

This cleaner should take care of most of your general cleaning needs. Mixed with liquid soap, the baking soda and borax will help to scour (without abrading surfaces), and the vinegar should cut through most of the grease. If you need more scrubbing power, add ordinary salt and baking soda (the salt may scratch more delicate surfaces). I can't seem to avoid inhaling the vapors ammonia gives off so I don't like to use it; but, a fourth of a cup of ammonia added to the solution also does the job. If you still need more cleaning power, try a little more elbow grease.

Window cleaner

Mix one part vinegar with five parts warm water. If the windows are very dirty, first wash them with soap and warm water.

Tub, Tile, and Sink cleaner

One-fourth cup of borax (or half that much baking soda) and 1 teaspoon of liquid soap mixed with 1 gallon of warm water should take care of most of the grime in the bathroom. Use a good stiff brush to scrub. For more strength, add 1 tablespoon ammonia.

Toilet bowl cleaner

Pour half a cup of borax and 1 teaspoon of liquid soap into your bowl and have at it with a good scrubber. If this doesn't do the job, add baking soda. Don't flush right away. Pour in a teaspoon of lemon juice and let the solution sit in the toilet for an hour.

Drain cleaner

Prevent drains from becoming clogged in the first place by putting a strainer or a hair trap in them, and occasionally cleaning it out. Once the drain is clogged, try a plunger or piece of bent wire; plumber's snakes are also good, but they're hard on pipes. If this doesn't work, dissolve 16 ounces of washing soda with 3 gallons of boiling water and pour it down the drain.

Floor cleaner

Most floors can be cleaned either with a mixture of borax (1/4 cup), liquid soap (1 teaspoon), and warm water (1 gallon); or a solution of washing soda (1/4 cup), distilled white vinegar (1/4 cup), and warm water (1 gallon).

Oven cleaner

You can clean most ovens with the all-purpose cleaner mentioned above. That, coupled with elbow grease, should be good enough to battle even the dirtiest of ovens. You can use ammonia to make the job a little easier. Pour half a cup of ammonia in a pan and leave it in the oven overnight to loosen up particles. For tougher ovens, turn on the oven to the warm setting for half an hour, turn it off, and place the dish of ammonia inside for the night. Open the oven door to let the vapors escape before you begin scrubbing the next day.

Furniture polish

Wood furniture polish can be made from a mixture of lemon oil (1 teaspoon) and mineral oil (1 pint), and applied with a rag. A handier polish can be put in a spray bottle. Mix olive oil (2 tablespoons), distilled white vinegar (1 tablespoon), and warm water (1 quart).

Carpet cleaner

An easy solution that will both clean and deodorize your carpet is cornmeal (2 cups) and borax (1 cup). Sprinkle it over the carpet and vacuum it up an hour later. Stains can be removed separately using warm water and soap.

Metal polisher

Copper can be cleaned with a lemon juice and salt mixture; brass with salt and flour. For silver, mix together baking soda (1 tablespoon), salt (1 tablespoon), and water (1 quart). Heat the solution and soak the silver piece in it for 3 minutes.

Air freshener

Rooms are kept smelling fresher if they are well ventilated. Vinegar in a dish works as a good freshener; it can be heated over a radiator to be even more effective. You can also put dried flowers in pots of water and heat the mixture.

Buy toxic-free cleansers

If mixing your own cleaning solutions is your idea of adding even more drudgery to house cleaning, buy cleansers that are already toxic free. Look at the list of ingredients on the product's label. If it has a POISON or DANGER label, with a list of precautions, it's better left on the shelf. Look for alternatives that tell you they're phosphate-free and biodegradable. Ecover brand household cleaners use non-polluting, organic ingredients that are phosphate-free. Among its products are dishwashing liquid, tub and tile cleaner, and toilet cleaner. Ecover products are available through Seventh Generation. Another company, Livos, offers non-toxic finishes, waxes, paints, and thinners. See the service directory for more information.

Handle toxic solutions with care

If you use toxic products, take some precautions. Warning labels don't tell you the whole story of a product's contents, but they give you an idea of how dangerous they really are. Wear protective clothing, such as gloves and goggles if directed, and don't breath in vapors. If you do inhale or ingest the contents, call a physician and bring the product with you if you go to the hospital. Don't use more of the product than the directions tell you; twice as much does not always give you twice as much cleaning power. And don't mix different products together. The combination, as with bleach and ammonia, can release toxic gases or cause explosions. Avoid all toxic products if you are pregnant.

Dispose of household toxics properly

When most people want to get rid of a toxic product, they usually throw it in the trash can, dump it down the drain, or pour it in the sewer. The toxic is out of the home, but it enters the ecosystem, seeping into the groundwater from landfills or entering bodies of water via treatment plants (which can't detoxify it). It poisons the environment and, eventually, returns to haunt us with contaminated water supplies.

The best way to get rid of toxic products is to take them to hazardous waste collection sites. With the help of the EPA, local governments have set up these sites, where citizens can dispose of such hazardous materials as motor oil, pesticides, and paint at no cost. Call your city hall for information on the locations of collection sites. Before you take the materials down there, first call your recycling center to see if it accepts any of the toxics. A number of centers will recycle motor oil, paint, and car batteries.

Use phosphate-free laundry detergents

Hard water, or water high in calcium and magnesium salts, does not mix well with soap. The salts prevent soap from attaching to dirt and grime, keeping clothes from getting clean. To solve this problem, manufacturers began adding phosphates to their detergents to "soften" the water, which then neutralizes the salts and allows soap to go about its cleaning job. Phosphates are great for the cleaning, but not so good for the lake or stream into which the "softened" water is eventually released, after it passes through a water-treatment plant, which is unable to restore it to its original state. Phosphates quickly kill whatever natural body of water they are in. The presence of phosphates in a lake accelerates the growth of algae, which, when it dies, provides a huge feast for ever-propigating micro-organisms. Their feeding frenzy slowly depletes the water of all its oxygen, suffocating all aquatic life and eventually killing the lake.

Phosphates are in many laundry detergents, even in areas where the water is already "soft" and doesn't need them. (To find out if your area has hard or soft water, call your city's Water Works Department). And even in areas with hard water, a low or phosphate-free detergent is usually available. Look at detergent boxes to determine the phosphate content. Don't be fooled. The number listed under the label "in the form of phosphates" is only 1/3 the real amount; multiply the percentage listed by 3 to get the true phosphate content. Liquid detergents are generally phosphate-free.

You can also make your own phosphate-free detergent. If you live in a soft water area, regular laundry soap flakes will work just fine. If you have hard water and have been using detergents, first wash your clothes in hot water and washing soda (1/4 cup) to remove detergent residues. This only needs to be done once, but don't forget to do it, or otherwise, your clothes will come out yellowed when washed with regular soap. Afterwards, wash them in regular soap flakes (1 1/2 cups) and washing soda (1/4 cup). From then on, simply use your homemade detergent.

Chlorine bleach

Most liquid bleach doesn't contain phosphates, but it can cause skin burns and eye injuries. It also releases extremely toxic fumes when mixed with ammonia or the acid found in tub and tile cleaners, so keep them separate. Use bleach in powder form instead, or use borax and baking soda.

Fabric softeners

A good replacement for fabric softeners is baking soda (1/4 cup) or distilled white vinegar (1/4 cup). Add it to the wash during the final rinse.

Use natural insecticides for household pests

That liquid which promises to kill cockroaches and ter-
mites could knock out more than pesky insects, it may be
harming you. Don't take chances with chemical insecticides when non-toxic, homemade substitutes made from
household ingredients will do.

Cockroaches

Keep cockroaches from ever entering your home by taping
up the cracks in walls, baseboards, and ducts. Sprinkling
borax around places where cockroaches enter your home
will also help. If this still doesn't work, set out Roach
Motels or make your own traps with bottles. Put some food
in the bottom of a bottle to attract cockroaches and grease
around the mouth to keep them from escaping.

Ants

Find out where ants are entering your house and squeeze
a lemon or lime into the hole. Leave the peels nearby.
Sprinkling talcum powder, cayenne pepper, or boric acid
at the entryway works as well.

Flies

Bagging flies with a fly-swatter or the rolled up end of a
newspaper is the quickest, most toxic-free method of getting rid of flies. A less energetic method is to make
homemade flypaper. Take a strip of brightly colored
paper, dip it in honey, and hang it from the ceiling. The
flies will be attracted by the bright color and the honey will
hold them when they land on it.

Fruit flies

Fruit flies, like regular houseflies, are attracted to light.
Place a dish of water underneath lightbulbs. The fruit flies
will be zapped when they land on the bulb and fall
stunned into the water, where they will drown. Another
method involves setting out a dish of beer. The flies are
attracted to the beer and drown in it.

Ticks and Fleas

These pests usually come into your home via your dog or
cat, so keep your pets clean. Wash your pets with soap and

water, and after drying them, spray on a herbal mixture of rosemary and water. Steep 1/2 cup of rosemary (fresh or dried) in a quart of boiling water. Pour the liquid into a pump bottle and spray onto your animal's coat. Let it dry. You can also grind up orange peels (not the fruit) in your blender, boil them in water and apply the solution to your pet.

Eliminate indoor air pollutants

Asbestos, formaldehyde, and radon are three of the most common indoor air pollutants. Present in everything from carpeting to insulation, they can cause coughing and, in severe cases, cancer.

Formaldehyde

Formaldehyde is almost as pervasive as the air in your house. It's a major ingredient in plywood and fiberboard, and can be found in the adhesives in drapes, carpeting, and wallpaper. The vapors won't kill you (you can't even smell them), but they can cause dizziness, nausea, and breathing problems. And since formaldehyde poisoning has only recently been discovered, no one knows what kind of damage a lifetime of sniffing in the vapors will do to you.

To determine how much formaldehyde your home has, order a test kit from 3-M. The kit, which costs about $50, contains a canister which reacts with formaldehyde and measures the amount of vapors in a room. For more information contact 3-M Monitors, A.F.S., P.O. Box 10752, White Bear, MN 55110; 612-426-0691. Besides removing formaldehyde-laden materials from your home, another way of reducing the vapors is to put out philodendrons and spider plants, which absorb formaldehyde.

Radon

Radon is an odorless, invisible gas that results from the radioactive decay of the uranium in rocks and soil. That's O.K. when it happens outside, but when the gas enters your house through cracks in your foundation, it's a different matter. When radon accumulates in the house, it can cause lung cancer through prolonged exposure. Tests done by the EPA indicate that 10% of all homes in the country have significant accumulations of radon.

Patching up cracks in basement floors can help reduce radon levels, but ventilation is even more important. Special ventilation systems are usually needed. To determine the radon level in your home, call your state health department and arrange for an inspection. For more information on radon, consult *Radon Reduction Methods* and *A Citizen's Guide to Radon*, both available from the EPA, Public Information Center, PM 211b, Washington, DC 20460.

Asbestos

Asbestos was a popular building material for homes constructed between the 1920s and 1970. And for good reason. The mineral was particularly effective in insulating, fireproofing, and roofing materials. The problem, however, is that when inhaled, asbestos fibers can scar lung tissue and eventually cause cancer. Asbestos as a building material has been banned since the early 1970s, but it is still present in many older homes. It poses no danger unless material containing asbestos is ripped or torn and the fibers enter the air. You can have your home inspected for asbestos by contacting the States Consumer Products Safety Commission, which, with the EPA, compiled a list of certified asbestos inspection companies. For a copy of the Asbestos List, write the States Consumer Products Safety Commission, Washington, DC 20207. An inspection will cost you anywhere from $500 to $2,000.

Keep your lawn toxic free

Over 300 million pounds of pesticides are applied to our lawns every year. That's a lot of toxic materials, many of them chemicals that can cause cancer, sterility, and kidney damage. And all to give the grass in our yards a manicured, golf course look. That artificial look was not always as desirable as it is today. When the author Nathaniel Hawthorne visited England in the mid-1800s he was horrified with the "bowling green" lawns characteristic of British homes, and couldn't wait to get back to American yards with their profusion of weeds, dandelions, and flowers. We can drastically cut our pesticide use by returning to that more natural vision of beauty.

If your vision of beauty can't be reconciled with a natural lawn, then try to achieve that manicured look without using chemical fertilizers. Plant grass that's adapted to the area. Kentucky bluegrass may look beautiful in your yard, but it needs a lot of water and is not as pest-resistant as other grasses. When you cut your grass, leave the clippings on the lawn. They serve as a natural compost, retaining moisture and providing roots with needed nutrients. The grass will grow fuller and in time force out more weeds. Rake the clippings only when accumulation begins to smother the lawn and prevent sun from reaching the grass. For more help, consult *The Chemical-Free Lawn* by Warren Schultz ($14.95 from Rodale Press).

Buy organic food

Every year, American farmers spray some 560 million pounds of pesticides on their crops to kill insects, retard spoilage, and most of all, to improve the products' appearance. Consequently, the food that makes it into our grocery stores is blemish-free and has a longer shelf life. But it is also expensive; it costs us the health of our land and our bodies. Besides actually cutting crop yields in half over the last forty years, pesticides have stripped land of its nutritional value, have contaminated lakes, streams, and groundwater supplies, and have poisoned up to a million people every year with their toxic residues.

Organic gardeners have long preached the wisdom of their methods. Using the basics of crop rotation, companion planting, and composting, natural gardeners for years have been producing bumper crops without the aid of chemical fertilizers or pesticides. A balance between using and renewing the soil's nutrients is struck, and healthy food results. Tomatoes are bright red on the inside and have real flavor when you bite into them, summer squash is a natural yellow. Lacking toxic residues, organic food is clean and safe, and the farming methods from which it is produced are good for the land.

Organically-grown produce can usually be found in health food stores, and is slowly making an appearance in regular grocery stores. It will cost you a few cents more, but the extra price gets you safe food and supports responsible agriculture. Also check out your local farmers' market. Many of the vendors sell organically grown food. (But be sure to ask first! Just because the food comes from a local farm does not necessarily mean it's pesticide free). Buying at farmers' markets is good on many levels. Since you're buying from local vendors, you're helping reduce the energy that's consumed to cart food across the country, and you're investing your money to support your area. To see if there is a farmers' market in your area, call city hall.

Grow your own organic food

The most enjoyable meal you'll ever eat is one that comes from your own garden. You are not eating a product that was bought in a store, you're literally eating the fruits of your nurturing and labor, something you had a hand in bringing to life. This is particularly true for food that's grown organically, since it demands more of your vigilance and effort to be brought up right.

There are lots of sources to help you set up your organic garden. One of the best places to begin is with organic garden guru, Robert Rodale. His Rodale Press puts out a number of books and publications that tell you everything you need to know about starting and maintaining an organic garden. *How to Grow Vegetables Organically* ($21.95) and *The Encyclopedia of Organic Gardening* ($34.95) are particularly useful. *Organic Gardening*, a monthly Rodale magazine, will keep you informed on the latest techniques, services, products, and advice for natural gardening. Subscriptions are $18/year. Contact Organic Gardening, Box 35, Emmaus, PA 18099; 215-967-5171.

Another source I highly recommend is Leo VanMeer's *Step-By-Step Guide to Natural Gardening*. Clear, engaging, and written in an easy-to-read style, this primer gives you the benefit of VanMeer's 70-odd years' experience with organic gardening. He sticks to the basics and doesn't assume any prior knowledge. Chapters discuss the choice of correct tools, improvement of soil fertility, companion planting, mulching, and container gardening, among other things. The book is $9.95 postpaid VanMeer Publishing Company, P.O. Box 2138 Clearwater, FL 34617; 813-531-6047.

Find the toxics being released in your community

If you suspect a company in your area is releasing toxics into the air or water, you can use a new law to find out what's going on. With access to TOXNET, a computerized toxicology data network, you can get all the information you need about the company, the pollutants it releases, and the effects those pollutants have on you and the environment.

TOXNET

Managed by the National Library of Medicine, TOXNET is a computerized storehouse of information on toxic substances. With data bank files such as Environmental Mutagen Information Center Backfile and Directory of Biotechnology Information Resources, TOXNET was obviously designed with the scientist in mind, not the average citizen. However, with a little effort, you can use this computer network to gain access to incredible amounts of information about the toxic substances being released into your community. The most valuable information for community activists is available under the Toxic Chemical Release Inventory database. Mandated by law to be available to the public through computer networks, the Inventory contains information on toxic chemicals being released into the environment, as well as the identity of the companies responsible. Other databases provide good information on the chemical substances themselves, such as their toxic effects, environmental fate, regulatory requirements and detection methods.

If you are not part of an organization, the best way to gain access to TOXNET is to go to a group already hooked up with it. Check with university hospitals, hospital libraries, or health professionals. Joining TOXNET yourself is expensive. There is no subscription or sign-up fee, but the prime time rate (Monday-Friday, 10:00 am to 5:00 pm, EST) is $25 an hour. Off-peak rates are $18.60 an hour. The costs for students are slightly lower. The databases are available 24-hours a day, seven days a week. For more information, contact the National Library of Medicine Specialized Information, Services Division, 8600 Rockville Pike, Bethesda, MD 20894; 301-496-6531 or 301-496-1131.

For more information

There are lots of resources out there if you need help with toxics. Some of the information for this chapter came from the Greenpeace publication, *Stepping Lightly on the Earth: Everyone's Guide to Toxics in the Home*, a good primer on alternatives to toxics. It's free; see Greenpeace in the environmental organization directory. Citizens for a Better Environment also puts out a fact sheet on toxic products and alternatives. Write to CBE, 33 East Congress, Suite 523, Chicago, IL 60605; 312-939-1530. One of the best books around is *A Guide to Hazardous Products Around the Home*, which is put out by the Household Hazardous Waste

Project. Send $5 to HHWP, Box 87, 901 South National Avenue, Springfield, MO 65804; 417-836-5777.

If you're interested in hooking up with groups dealing with toxics, contact the Citizen's Clearinghouse for Hazardous Waste, the Lois Gibbs organization. For more information, see the environmental directory. Another good group is Coalition for Alternatives to Pesticides (NCAP). The organization sells information packets ($10 to $15), factsheets ($1.00), and books that tell you everything you need to know about pesticides, alternatives, and political strategies to fight polluters. Its quarterly newsletter, *Journal of Pesticide Reform*, will keep you up to date on the fight for pesticide reform. Membership to NCAP is $25/year. Contact: NCAP, P.O. Box 1393, Eugene, OR 97440; 503-344-5044.

Founded after the death of Rachel Carson, the Rachel Carson Council has established itself as a resource center for people who need information on environmental issues, especially those which involve chemical contamination, the problem explored in *Silent Spring*. They have a good collection of books, periodicals and subjects files for use by the public. Contact: Rachel Carson Council, Inc., 8940 Jones Mill Road, Chevy Chase, MD 20815; 301-652-1877.

National Coalition Against the Misuse of Pesticides is a leader in trying to change policies regarding pesticides. They serve as a support group to local organizations, and have a toxicologist on staff who is available to answer questions. Contact NCAMP, 530 7th St., SE, Washington, DC 20003; 202-542-5450.

Pesticide Action Network is a networking coalition of over 300 groups working against toxic pollution. It maintains extensive files in its information clearinghouse. A recent campaign centered on replacing pesticides with ecologically sound alternatives. For more information, contact: North America Regional Center, P.O. Box 610, San Francisco, CA 94101; 415-541-9140.

"Comes down: raindrops like pellets splattering on the rock, knocking the berries off the junipers, plastering my shirt to my back, drumming on my hat like hailstones and running in a waterfall off the brim."

Ed Abbey, *Desert Solitaire*

CHAPTER 5

WATER CONSERVATION
STOPPING THE DRAIN ON A VALUABLE RESOURCE

By the time you are out the door and on your way to work in the morning, you've used over 100 gallons of water. Think back over your morning routine: you take a long, hot shower (there's 80 gallons already) and then brush your teeth (6 gallons). If you shave, add another 10 gallons. Somewhere in there you use the toilet (6 gallons). In the kitchen you use water to make the orange juice and coffee, rinse off your dishes, and wipe off the counter (3 gallons). You use the toilet one more time (6 gallons again), and are off. Total: 101 gallons, 111 for shavers. Of course, the exact total will vary with each individual, but it's not hard for even the most water-conscious person to use up to a 100 gallons; most of us can think of things we do in our routine that use up even more.

This is just the morning. To figure out the amount of water you use during the rest of the day, add at least another 70 gallons. At that rate, you go through 1,197 gallons of water in a week, 4,788 in a month, 57,456 in a year. And this is being repeated by millions of people across the country every day.

The point is not for us to feel guilty about our water use. We all need water to live and carry on with our daily lives. But there are many things we can do to dramatically cut back on the amount of water we use. Some are easy, like turning off the water when brushing our teeth; others require more of an effort and some sacrifice, such as installing low-flow shower heads and reducing the blast of that morning shower. Water is one of our most precious resources and, as several circumstances have shown us--the drought of 1988, water pollution, and mandatory water rationing in many areas on occasion--it's a resource we can ill afford to take for granted.

Wash dishes by hand instead of in a dishwasher

This one is in some ways a judgment call. If you wash dishes in one basin and rinse them in another, you should be able to hand wash a meal's worth or more of dishes with only 10 gallons of water. Standard dishwashers use 14 gallons of water per load. Thus, washing dishes by hand appears to be more water-efficient than using a dishwasher. But there's no way you could hand wash with 10 gallons of water the number of dishes a full dishwasher can clean with 14. At least I can't, not without ending up with some pretty grungy-looking dishes. So, it's better to hand wash small to medium loads; but for large loads, you'll go through less water using a dishwasher.

There's another consideration here: mechanical dishwashers use up electricity, while human dishwashers work by the sweat of the brow--a renewable and non-polluting energy resource. Which is better, wasting water or wasting electricity? It's your call. We wash dishes by hand because we like the ability to control the water flow and because we don't want another energy-gobbling appliance in our kitchen. If you use a dishwasher, though, make sure to use it as efficiently as possible (see below).

Fill your dishwasher before using

Your dishwasher uses the same amount of water (14 gallons) to wash three cups as it does to do a whole load, so make sure you only run it when it's full. To save even more water, scrape your dishes instead of rinsing them off.

Don't wash dishes when the water's running

If you wash dishes by hand, don't wash them while the water is running. You use up to between 20 to 30 gallons of water that way, depending on the size of the job. Wash the dishes in one basin and rinse them in another, a method that uses about 10 gallons of water. If you still want to rinse the dishes off with free-flowing tap water, install a faucet aerator with an on/off lever.

Turn off the water when brushing your teeth, washing your face, and shaving

The water doesn't need to be on while the toothbrush is in your mouth or while the razor is removing those whiskers. Sure, it's a pain to turn the faucet off and on, but you can save a lot of water if you do. With the tap flowing continuously, you use 6 gallons of water when you're brushing your teeth and between 8 and 12 gallons when shaving. Turning the water off can cut that volume down to a trickle.

Install faucet aerators

Faucet aerators are devices that screw into faucet heads to restrict the amount of water flowing out of them. Most faucets use 3 to 4 gallons per minute (g.p.m.), but by mixing air in with the water, aerators are able to reduce the rate of flow to anywhere from .5 to 2.5 g.p.m. Many also come with an on/off lever which allows you to turn off the water and then turn it back on without having to readjust for temperature. Seventh Generation and Resources Conservation sell aerators which use 60% less water than normal heads, and are equipped with on/off controls for under $10. For $6.95 Rising Sun sells a kitchen faucet aerator with a flow rate of 2.5 g.p.m. and an on/off lever. See the service directory. Also check your local plumbing and hardware store.

Repair leaky faucets

Most of the time, repairing a leaky faucet is only a matter of screwing off the handle and replacing a worn washer. Total work time is ten minutes; the cost of a new washer is pennies. It's costing you a lot more *not* to fix it. A steady drip could be wasting as much as 25 gallons of water a day. Even if it's just a drip every second or so, you're losing some 650 gallons of water over the course of a year.

Take a shower instead of a bath

An average shower uses half the water that a bath does. To see for yourself, plug up the tub while showering and see how much water you use. More than likely, the tub isn't even close to being filled. If it is, then you need to take a shorter shower or install a low-flow shower head (see below). If you just can't give up on a bath, then fill it up only halfway.

Install a low-flow shower head

The luxurious shower you took this morning used up anywhere from 60 to 100 gallons of water. That's a lot of water, but it's hard to imagine starting the day without a good, long dousing. You can have the shower and cut water use at the same time by installing a low-flow shower head. While regular shower heads allow 6 to 10 gallons of water to pass through per minute, low-flow heads restrict that flow to 2 g.p.m. That's saving 4 times the amount of water, but since the water is mixed with air, the pressure is just as strong as with normal heads. You're also using less hot water, which saves on energy.

One good feature on many of the new models is an on/off control, which allows you to turn off the water at the shower head. This lets you shampoo and lather up without having to cut the water off at its source and then waste more water readjusting the hot/cold mix when you're ready to rinse. Real Goods Trading Company, Seventh Generation, and Resources Conservation all sell low-flow shower heads with on/off controls for under $20 (this usually just includes the shower head itself, not the arm that attaches the head to the wall). Seventh Generation and Resources Conservation offer the colorful Europa brand (Resources Conservation also has its own Incredible Heads line); Real Goods' "Nova" shower head uses only 2.1 g.p.m., which can be reduced to 1.1 g.p.m. in return for a lower pressure. See the service directory. Also check your local plumbing or hardware store.

Put a water displacer in your toilet tank

Every time you flush your toilet, anywhere from 5 to 7 gallons of water rushes down the drain. Your toilet doesn't need half that to do the job. Cut back on water waste by dropping a water displacer in the bottom of your toilet tank. It can be anything that takes up space and displaces water that would normally be flushed out. In the past, I've used bricks or the bottom half of a Clorox bottle. The brick takes up space water would normally fill; the bottom of the Clorox bottle fills with water and prevents it from flowing out. I like them not only because they displace about 25% of the water, but also because they are inexpensive. Fancier, high-tech ones have recently been appearing. Seventh Generation sells a "toilet dam," a rubber device that displaces up to four gallons of water. It's $6.50.

Install a low-flush toilet

Low-flush toilets reduce by 60% to 90% the amount of water normally used for flushing. The Aqualine, a sleek, European-looking model, uses only 1-1/2 gallons per flush, and the Sealand China Toilet uses less than a pint, about the volume of a grade school milk carton! That's a big savings on the 5 to 7 gallons of water per flush used by standard models. Real Goods Trading Company offers the two models mentioned above, priced from $175 to $300. They are easy to install and attach to regular plumbing fixtures. Eljer also manufactures the Ultra I, which uses 1-1/4 gallons of water per flush. Contact: Eljer, Three Gatway Center, Pittsburgh, PA, 15222.

Install a composting toilet

Granted, this is one for the really committed, but it's not as gross or as complicated as you might think. Here's how it works. Your toilet sits on top of or is connected to a tank, which collects your waste (and other organic materials, depending on the model) and turns it into compost. Liquid wastes evaporate into water vapor, which is vented outside through a pipe; solid wastes become compost, which you remove from the tank one to four times a year and add to your garden. The venting system prevents odor, and the only work required involves throwing in a handful of peat moss and turning the handle a couple of times a week to aerate the compost. And since each flush uses less than a pint of water, composting toilets don't waste valuable resources. Some energy in the form of electrically-powered heaters and fans may be needed for the larger models (to quicken evaporation), but many don't require any electricity at all. Real Goods Trading Company offers a number of composting toilets ranging in price from $1,000 to $5,000.

Don't leave the water on when washing your car

While you are soaping up your car, that garden hose is blasting 5 to 8 gallons of water down the driveway every minute. At that rate, you could easily go through 120 gallons of water to wash just one car. So, turn the hose off when you're not actually using it to rinse the suds off the car. Better yet, attach a spray nozzle to save the water that's lost when you're going back and forth to the faucet. With a little efficiency, you can wash your car with only 10 to 15 gallons of water. Save even more by washing your car only when absolutely necessary.

Sweep instead of hose off driveways and sidewalks

I've seen this one a lot, and have been guilty of it myself: using water pressure instead of broom action to clean off driveways, patios, and sidewalks. It's fast, easy, and kind of fun, and it does a much better job than a broom could ever do. It's also incredibly wasteful. Just multiply the number of minutes you have the water on times 8, and you'll get a good idea of how many gallons of water you use. Total water use for sweeping: 0.

Water plants and lawns in the evening

When you water your lawn during the day, heat causes some of the water to evaporate. Watering in the cool of the evening allows more of the water to actually soak into the ground and reach plant roots.

Buy plants native to the area

Before you throw new grass seed onto your struggling lawn, make sure it's adapted to the environment. Bushes, trees, grass--any type of plant--that are native to the area require less water to flourish. In some cases, they need only half the amount of water that foreign plants do. To find out which plants are best for your area, contact your local nursery, arboretum, or gardening club.

Get more information

Rocky Mountain Institute, a "resource policy center," publishes a number of good booklets on water conservation. One, "Water Efficiency for Your Home: Products Which Save Water, Energy, and Money," provides practical advice in choosing and installing water-efficient fixtures in your home. Contact RMI for ordering details. For more information on RMI and its work, see the service directory.

"Such prosperity as we have known it up to present is the consequence of rapidly spending the planet's irreplaceable capital."

CHAPTER 6

SAVING ENERGY
USING LESS AND USING IT WISELY

Part of the reason we're not more energy-conscious is that we don't have to generate the energy ourselves. If we had to shovel coal or throw wood into a furnace every time we wanted to have power to watch TV, turn on the lights, or cook a meal we might think harder about how to use that energy wisely. Maybe we'd plan more, cooking a couple of dishes in a hot oven at the same time, or be more stingy by taking shorter showers or turning the heat down at night. If we had to mine that coal or chop that wood ourselves and drag it home, well, I'm sure our energy consumption would drop dramatically and we'd spend a lot more of our time talking about practical ways to save energy.

But at the flip of a switch or the turn of a dial, energy is magically and instantly delivered. We don't think of where it came from or what resources are being used up to create it, or even what kind of pollution is being generated because of it. We are removed, physically and emotionally, from the power plant, and out of sight is truly out of mind. But just because we can't see it doesn't mean that mountains aren't being ravaged by strip mining or oil isn't being drawn out of the bowels of the earth. Every once in a while we are confronted with the pollution that our need for energy creates: a tanker spills millions of gallons of oil into pristine waters, or radioactive wastes are spewed into the air when the core of a nuclear power generator melts down. Our anxiety lasts about as long as the media coverage, and we rarely recognize the connection between environmental catastrophes and our leaving the lights on in every room of the house. But that connection is very real. So, the next time you turn on your lights, imagine what it would be like to power them yourself, and think about the dwindling resources that are being used to generate the energy and the pollution that comes with it.

Audit your home's energy use

You'll know how to save energy once you know how you are using it. A complete energy audit is the best way to start. There are a few ways to handle this. First, call your local utility. Some utility companies employ energy specialists, who will walk through your home and suggest ways of improving its energy efficiency. A few companies, like Central Maine Power, will even pay for or subsidize improvements (don't get your hopes up too high for this, though). Audits performed by utilities are usually free, but you can't always count on getting a top-notch inspection. To get the most out of a free inspection, prepare in advance a list of questions to ask the energy specialist about specific areas in your home. More reliable audits can be had through private energy firms, but they can run you a couple hundred dollars. To locate a private energy firm, look under "energy conservation services" in the Yellow Pages. Call around to get the best deal, and make sure you know exactly what each company does and does not look for.

Or, you can do an energy audit yourself. It may not be as extensive as one offered by a private company, but it will open your eyes to just how much energy your home is wasting. And the price is tough to beat. The sections below will show you the problems to look for and how to fix them.

INSULATION

Almost half the energy used to keep our homes warm in the winter and cool in the summer escapes through countless leaks in places such as windows, walls, and attics. Closing up these holes can save hundreds of dollars in energy costs during the course of a year. To locate drafts, place a candle at different locations throughout your house (such as by windows and baseboards), and watch the movement of the flame.

Caulk and weatherstrip windows and doors

Between 15% to 25% of a home's heating and cooling is lost through leaky doors and windows. Caulking can seal off cracks along joints and edges. Make sure to get a good caulk compound (such as siliconized caulk) that will adhere well and not dry out after only a few months. Apply weatherstripping around door and window frames. To get the most mileage out of it, read the directions and apply carefully. Caulk and weatherstripping are not that expensive, and they can save you up to 10% on your energy bills.

Install storm windows or low-emissivity windows

You can cut down on heat loss by putting plastic over your windows, but installing storm windows is a more permanent and efficient solution. It's an investment of a few hundred dollars, but you can save up to 15% on your heating bills over the course of a year. Also look into low-emissivity, or low-e, windows. These double-pane windows work on an improved greenhouse principle. A transparent coating on the window allows the sun to pass through, but doesn't let the heat escape, as other windows do. Up to 25% more heat is retained. Low-e windows are available through most window manufacturers.

Insulate

Insulating is an easy way of reducing your home's energy use by 20% to 30%. But before you head off to the home improvement center, make sure you know what you're doing. Take a careful inventory of areas you want to insulate and what kind of materials you'll need. Look carefully at crawl spaces, ceilings, attics, rooms over garages, and outside walls. Insulating pads, or batts, are usually made from glass fiber and can be tacked or set into place; loose insulation made from fiberglass or cellulose can be blown in. Before you buy the materials, look on the packaging for the R-value, the number which rates its effectiveness (the higher the R-value, the higher its effectiveness). Insulating can be complicated, so don't be afraid to ask for help. Talk to a building inspector or to your utility company, or consult home repair manuals for more concrete information. The Massachusetts Audubon Society publishes a set of helpful booklets on home energy efficiency, two of which deal specifically with insulation, "All About Insulation" and "Superinsulation." They're $3.50 apiece, available from Massachusetts Audubon Society, Public Information Office, Lincoln, MA 01773; 617-259-9500.

Close off unused rooms

Don't waste energy by heating or cooling rooms you don't use or spend much time in. In rooms you don't use, such as bedrooms and dining rooms, close the doors and shut off vents. In the summertime pull down the blinds or close the drapes; in the winter, keep blinds and drapes open in sunny rooms.

Close off your fireplace

As much of 8% of your heating escapes through a chimney when the flue is open. Enjoy the fire, but close the flue when the fire's out for the day. Even when the fire's burning, a lot of your home's electrical or gas heat is sucked up the chimney. You can install glass doors on the front of your fireplace, which keep more of the heat in the room. Granted, this may mar the aesthetics of an open fire, but, in this case, aesthetics don't do much to lower your heating bills. Lastly, when a fire is going, turn down your thermostat.

HEATING

Half of your home's energy is used for heating. Insulating will go a long way toward cutting back on that energy use, but there are additional steps you can take to save even more.

Clean off registers and vents

Dust and debris on a register can absorb and block heat that would otherwise warm a room. Also make sure furniture is placed away from registers to insure unimpeded delivery of heat.

Turn down the thermostat

Turning your thermostat up a couple of degrees may not seem like such a big deal, but it's increasing your energy bill up to 3% per degree. To save energy without freezing, set your thermostat to 65 degrees during the day and lower it to 60 at night. Thermostats on automatic timers can do the job for you. And don't keep fiddling with the dial. A system that is constantly readjusting to different settings uses up more energy and warms a house less efficiently. Drafts near the thermostat can also play havoc with your heating system, unnecessarily heating up your house when only the area around the thermostat is cool. Make sure the location of your thermostat approximates the conditions of your whole house. Keep it out of direct sunlight, away from heating ducts and registers, and well away from frequently used doors.

Use space heaters

Placing space heaters in rooms you often use allows you to turn down the thermostat and takes some pressure off your central heating system. Heaters are especially good if you tend to live in a few rooms, such as a kitchen or the living room. Space heaters can be big energy users, so only use a few of them at a time; if you need too many, you're probably better off with your main unit.

Wear warm clothing

This is a little like Ronald Reagan's quip that energy conservation means being cold in the winter and hot in the summer. But the point of wearing warm clothing is not so much to deal with cold due to lowered thermostats, but to enable you to turn your thermostat down. If you're in warm clothes you need less heat. This means, obviously, that if you're using energy responsibly, you probably won't be able to walk around in short pants and a tee shirt without being cold.

Use a humidifier

Your dry skin will tell you that there's not much moisture in the air when the temperature is cold. A humidifier puts moisture back into the air and makes it easier for your body to handle colder temperatures. If your home is heated by radiators, simply place pans of water on the units, thus putting your energy consumption to double use.

Turn the heat way down when you go to bed

This repeats a little the thought about lowering your thermostat at night, but I'm talking about turning it *way* down. Not enough to freeze the water in your pipes and burst them, but enough to make you add lots of blankets on your bed and think twice about getting out of the warmth in the middle of the night to use the bathroom. Blankets and your body heat will keep you plenty warm, so before you go to bed, turn it down.

Get the most out of your furnace

Your furnace is the heart of your heating system, so improvements in energy efficiency will be severely limited if it's not in top form. Before the beginning of the winter season, have your furnace inspected and maintenanced by a professional (under "heating contractors" in the Yellow Pages). Insulate and tape pipes and ducts, and replace the air filter once a month. Installing an automatic timer will insure that your thermostat is set to the right temperature at the right time. In the off season, turn off the pilot light.

If you're looking to replace your furnace (not a bad idea if it's older than 20 years), look into gas units. They are among the most energy-efficient. If you want to upgrade an electric system, think about getting a heat pump, which takes heat present in the air outside and transfers it into the house. They're not cheap (anywhere from $500 to $2,000), but they can reduce your electricity use by 40%. For more information, invest $3.50 in "Heating Systems," a good primer on caring for and understanding furnaces. Contact: Massachusetts Audubon Society, Public Information Office, Lincoln, MA 01173; 617-259-9500.

COOLING

Some of the recommendations here are based on the same principles as those listed above for heating. Insulating, closing off rooms and keeping equipment in good running order, apply equally well to cooling as to heating. There are, however, a number of other ideas which can cut your cooling bills by an additional 10% to 30%.

Plant trees

Properly placed, broadleaf shade trees can cool rooms by as much as 20 degrees. If trees are planted on the south side of the house the leaves will block the sun in the summer; in the winter when their leaves have fallen, they will allow the sun to enter and warm the house. Don't plant trees too close to your house, and remember to choose trees that are indigenous to your area. Contact your local arboretum or tree-planting organization for more information.

Keep heat out of the house

Keeping your home as cool as possible through natural means will lessen your need for air conditioning. You can do this in a number of obvious ways. Light bulbs are small heat generators; keep lights off unless you absolutely need them. Close blinds and drapes when the sun is shining through the windows. Blinds with a reflective coating can reduce the amount of radiation entering a window by 80%. Avoid using heat-producing appliances, such as dryers and ovens, and if you must, use them during the cooler part of the day.

Install kitchen and bathroom fans

Fans above the stove can draw off some of the local excess heat, reducing the strain on your main system. A bathroom fan can do the same thing. Turn it on after showering or bathing and wait a few minutes before opening the door and allowing cool air to enter.

Use window units when possible

Individual window units are usually more effective and energy-efficient than a central air conditioning system. But make sure you get an energy-efficient unit. First, select a unit that's equipped to cool the room in which it's to be used. Units that are too small will forever be trying to cool spacious rooms; big units, on the other hand, will waste energy by sending a smaller room into a deep freeze. Look at the unit's efficiency. The efficiency of an air conditioner is measured by its energy efficiency rating (EER), a number reflecting its cooling capacity (measured by BTUs) as compared to its power needs (measured by watts). The higher the EER, the higher a unit's efficiency. Anything over 9 is considered very efficient. EERs are usually imprinted on a plate somewhere on the unit, but you can figure it out yourself by dividing the BTUs by the watts needed.

You can further improve an air conditioner's efficiency by regularly cleaning its filter (located in front of the fan) and keeping the unit out of the direct line of the sun. If you've got a big area to cool, use a fan to spread the coolness throughout the room. And if you're going out for an extended period, turn the unit off.

Raise thermostats in central air systems

There's nothing like walking into your house on a hot, muggy day and being greeted by a blast of cold air. The colder the better. But to be energy-efficient, set your thermostat to 78 degrees. It's not going to send a shiver down your spine when you open your door, but it will still be cooler than the outside, and you'll be comfortable. Raise the thermostat even higher when you leave the house for extended periods.

If your air has been off all day, don't set it to a low temperature, thinking it will cool the house down quicker. Your system takes the same amount of time to reach 78 degrees regardless of whether the thermostat is set to 78 or 60. The lower setting will just make your system work longer, because you'll probably forget to turn the thermostat back up once the temperature reaches 78.

Locate thermostats away from heating sources

A thermostat turns on and off based on the temperature in its vicinity, so place your thermostat in a location that approximates the conditions of your house. Keep it out of direct sunlight and away from lamps, televisions, and other heat-generating appliances.

Keep registers and vents clear

Dust, drapes, and furniture on and over registers can hinder your central air system from delivering cold air efficiently. When I was a kid, our curtains partially draped over our vent, and I can remember standing behind the curtains because the area between them and the window was the coolest place in the house. The rest of the living room was hot, but the 4" by 4" spot behind the drapes was a cool 65 degrees. Your whole house will be cooler if your registers are clean and unobstructed.

Use a dehumidifier

In the summer you feel the hottest when both temperature and humidity is high. Moisture in the air makes it more difficult for your body to cool itself through evaporation. Dehumidifiers remove that moisture from the air for you, making you feel cooler. They also take a load off air conditioners, which struggle to lower both temperatures and humidity. With some of their work done for them, air conditioners can be turned down.

Install a vent fan in the attic

If you've ever gone into an attic in the middle of summer you know how much heat is retained there. A vent fan draws off some of the heat and takes a load off your main air system, lowering attic temperatures by as much as 35 degrees.

Get the most out of your central air system

Central air units can be made more efficient in much the same way that furnaces can: keep the machinery in good working order through yearly inspections and maintenance. Insulate vents and ducts, especially in unprotected areas of your home, and change filters every month or so. Clean and remove debris from around outside coils and fans.

If you're in the market to buy a new system, talk to a specialist about a unit that has a capacity which matches your needs. And look at its rating. Central air systems are rated, much like window units, by their Seasonal Energy Efficiency Ratio (SEER), a comparison of output to energy use. Most systems have a SEER of 9, but new laws will require a SEER of 10 by 1992.

LAUNDRY

Washers and dryers are energy guzzlers that are used at all times of the year. Washers, in particular, place a strong demand on resources, using on average 40 gallons of water per load and requiring energy to fuel both the machine and the hot water heater. That adds up for the average family, which does four or five loads of laundry every two weeks. Dryers, which run much longer than washers to do their job, demand almost as much energy.

Washing

Do full loads

This doesn't mean cramming your washer so full of dirty clothes that it rocks back and forth during the spin cycle, but it does mean combining smaller loads or waiting to do a wash until you've got a good pile of dirty clothes. Doing full loads saves on water and on the energy it takes to run both your washer and your hot water heater, two of the biggest energy drainers in the house. Be careful though; loads that are too big result in wrinkled and partially clean clothes, which just means that you have to do them twice.

Presoak dirty laundry

Some machines have soak cycles which do this for you, but if not, pull out your really dirty clothes and let them soak before throwing them into the washer. It will save you, and the machine, from doing them more than once.

Wash with cold or warm water when possible

Many of your clothes can be done in cold water. In fact, some machines, as well as a number of detergents, are specifically designed to wash clothes in cold water. Your water heater, which accounts for up to 20% of your home's energy use, will get a break that could save you a lot of money over the course of a year.

Don't use too much detergent

Pouring in more detergent than is recommended on the directions doesn't get your clothes cleaner. It actually makes your machine work harder to do the same job.

Use a James hand washing machine

This is one step up from washing your clothes down at the river and beating them against the rocks, but you won't find a more energy-efficient machine around. The James hand washer is essentially a barrel split lengthwise and set on legs. Water is added to the tub and a hand-powered agitator removes dirt from the clothes. Believe it or not, people still use them. The James machine offered by Real Goods ($175) is made of galvanized metal and lined with fiberglass to reduce wear. A hand wringer, which attaches to the edge, removes more water from clothes than does the spin cycle on a standard washer.

A step up from the James machine is the Speed Queen wringer washer, an electric washing machine that uses only 800 watts of power and half the water of regular washers. Part of the savings is due to the fact that it has no spin cycle--wet clothes are pulled through the wringer on top of the machine. Available for $550 from Real Goods Trading Company.

Drying

Dry clothes on a clothesline

Fresh air is a lot cheaper to use than electrically generated heat, and it leaves clothes smelling and feeling more natural. If you don't want to dry all your clothes on a line, then hang those that require a lot of heat to dry, such as jeans, towels, and blankets.

Fill clothes dryers

The same amount of heat in a dryer goes to drying a pair of socks as it does a whole load of laundry, so when you use your dryer fill it to its capacity. But don't put in more wet laundry than the dryer can handle. You won't save money by stuffing four or five loads into one machine. The drum may rotate and the heat may pour in, but the dryer is straining to do the job, and you'll need to keep it running longer. You'll also end up pulling out a lot of wrinkled clothes when the cycle is done.

Dry heavy and light clothing separately

While heavy laundry, like pants and towels, is still drying, the lighter laundry in the load--underwear, tee shirts, socks--is probably already dry. Use your dryer more efficiently by sorting laundry into two piles according to weight and drying them separately. And make sure to put the dryer on the right setting. Light loads don't need to be dried on the "hot" setting.

Use automatic dry cycle

You can probably think of a few times when you turned your dryer on and forgot to go back to it until hours later. Your dryer will waste a lot of energy pouring heat onto clothes that are already dry. The automatic dry cycle works on a timer that stops the dryer when the cycle is through.

Keep lint screen clean

That blanket of soft dust over the lint screen can hinder the flow of air circulating in the drum, making the dryer work harder. Remove the lint after each load.

Hang clothes to be ironed in the shower

Save a little on time, electricity, and arm-power. The next time you take a shower, hang clothes to be ironed in the bathroom. The warm water vapor from the shower will take the wrinkles out (this works best for light-weight clothing).

LIGHTING

There are over 2.5 billion light bulb sockets in the country, and it doesn't take much imagination to see that an enormous load of energy is generated to keep the bulbs burning. We can have just as much light for a fraction of the energy by making a few simple changes.

Turn off lights when you don't need them

Keeping a light on in every room of the house may make going from room to room easier and less spooky, but it wastes a lot of electricity. When you walk out of a room, turn the light off. And although burning lights may make your house look warm and inviting, turn off both indoor and outdoor lights when you leave home unless they are absolutely needed. If you feel you need outside lights on for protection, consider installing automatic flood lights, which turn on when motion is detected (see below).

Dust off light bulbs and lamp shades

Chances are that if you run your finger across any non-enclosed light bulb (not when it's on!) in your house, you'll cut a trail through a coating of dust. It may not look like much, but that dust is absorbing some of the light emitted by the bulb. Dusting bulbs, globes, and lamp shades will increase the brightness and effectiveness of your lighting.

Use low wattage light bulbs whenever possible

There are some areas of your house that need bright lighting, such as libraries, kitchens, and work areas. Installing high wattage bulbs in these places makes sense. But use lower watt bulbs in other areas not so dependent on bright light. Don't install a 75- or 100-watt bulb in hallways, closets, basements, or on the front porch, where a 40-watt bulb will do. Go around your home and determine your real lighting needs.

Use lamps with three-way switches and dimmers

There might be some places where lighting needs vary according to what's going on there. We have lights in our living room, for instance, which are used both for general lighting and for reading. A 40-watt bulb is fine for the first purpose, but it doesn't emit enough light to read by comfortably. In places such as this, install lamps with three-way sockets (watts of 60, 75, 100), using the setting that's best for the job. Make sure to turn it down to a lower setting after finishing a job which requires brighter light.

Dimmers serve the same purpose for overhead lighting. We had dimmers in the lights over our dining room table, and turned the lights down during meals and up for card games. Both dimmers and three-way sockets can be found in hardware stores (don't forget the three-way bulbs). They are very easy to install, even for the most non-mechanical of us.

Use photoelectric cells or timers

Many street lights are attached to photoelectric cells, which turn lights on when sunlight disappears and off when it reappears. There are a bunch of consumer products using photoelectric technology, including indoor night lights and exterior flood lights. You can find them at most hardware stores. Timers are central clocks, which you can set to turn lights off and on automatically at specific times. Make sure you adjust the timer for seasonal changes in daylight time.

Use fluorescent lighting

Fluorescent lights have come a long way from the bright white, buzzing tubes in the ceilings of your high school hallways. The light is more natural in color and the irritating flickering and buzzing has diminished. They do a much better job at illuminating an area than a standard bulb, and with less energy. One of those long white tubes will cost you 10 times more than a regular bulb, but it gives off more than twice as much light as its incandescent counterpart and requires half as much energy. It also lasts nearly 11,000 hours longer. Fluorescent lighting is especially good in the kitchen and in garage work areas.

Buy compact fluorescent or halogen light bulbs

Regular light bulbs, or incandescent lamps, as they are known in the business, haven't changed much since Edison invented them in 1879: an enclosed filament converts electricity into heat and light. Improvement through the years has resulted in an inexpensive bulb which emits a steady glow of "warm" light for months at a time, but it's not much more efficient than Edison's original lamp. Most of the electricity powering the bulb goes into generating heat, not light--just touch a light bulb after it has been on a minute or two. Ninety percent of the electricity went into burning your finger; only 10% produced the light. Replace those energy hogs with compact fluorescent or halogen bulbs.

Compact fluorescent lamps

Compact fluorescent bulbs are constructed in a way that produces less heat and more light. The lamp is filled with mercury, which, when charged with electricity, excites the phosphorescent coating on the inside of the tube to emit light. The resulting efficacy rate--the output of the light versus the watts needed to produce it--puts the regular bulb to shame. Compact fluorescents using 11-, 15-, and 20-watts emit the same light as their 40-, 60-, and 75-watt counterparts. And they last ten times longer than the standard light bulbs, good for 10,000 burning hours apiece.

They are more expensive up front. A regular light bulb costs you 75 cents; a compact fluorescent will run $20 to $28, including the ballast (an energy-saving base into which you insert the fluorescent bulb). Before you nix the idea of spending $20 on a light bulb, consider the amount of money you'll save with a bulb that uses 70% less energy than a regular one and last 10 times longer. Using 55 fewer watts and lasting 13 times longer than a standard 75-watt bulb, a 20-watt, $25.95 Dulux El compact fluorescent lamp will save you $2.47 for every 1,000 hours of operation. Multiply that savings by all the bulbs in your house.

Compact fluorescents are the way to go, but there are a few things to keep in mind before rushing out to get some. The bulbs come in different shapes and sizes, and your lamp shade may not completely hide some of the taller ones. You may have to buy a special extender for a few dollars to match things up. Also, not all bulbs can be used with dimmer switches, and they are not designed for especially cold or hot weather.

Halogen Lamps

A halogen, or quartz, lamp is much like a regular incandescent bulb, except that halogen gas surrounds the filament, creating a brighter light when burned. For each watt used, the halogen lamp produces 10% more light than its incandescent counterpart and lasts about three times longer.

Halogens cost three to five times as much as regular bulbs. Because they produce a bright, white light, halogens are especially good for directed light, such as for reading and sewing. Another benefit halogens have is that, although they emit a bright light, it is still soft, not harsh and glaring. However, they are heavier than standard bulbs and may cause lightweight lamps to become top heavy. Real Goods Trading Company sells a wide range of halogens, including a popular brand which looks just like an incandescent lamp ($12). They also carry halogen flood lamps and desk lights. Rising Sun features a halogen floor lamp ($190) and reading light ($22).

Where to get compact fluorescent and halogen lamps

You probably won't find these lamps in your local hardware store. Some specialty stores may carry them, however. Look under "lighting" or "light" in your Yellow Pages. You can get them through the mail from Real Goods Trading Company, Rising Sun, and Seventh Generation (see service directory). Some utility companies offer compact fluorescent and halogen lamps (as well as other low-energy brands) for free or at a discount. Whether you're looking for compact fluorescent or halogen lamps, be discerning about what you buy. The information on a lamp's energy-saving capacity can be misleading and overstated. To learn more about buying fluorescent lighting, read Rising Sun's "Energy-Efficient Lighting and Water Efficient Technology for the Home" ($3), an easy-to-read consumer's guide. Real Goods' *Alternative Energy Sourcebook* ($10) also has a lot of good information on energy-efficient lighting.

Install automatic flood lights

Within each of these flood lights is an infrared sensor, which detects movement or heat within 50 to 75 feet. The lights remain off until a large object, such as a person or a car, comes within its range. Only then do the flood lights come on. You save electricity and get a visual warning that something has entered your yard. Hardware stores carry these lights, but you can get a solar powered one for $400 from Real Goods. A solar panel on top of the lighting box collects sun during the day, storing it for nighttime use.

Use solar-powered outdoor lights

If you live in a particularly sunny area, you can power your outdoor lights for free. Solar panels absorb sun during the day, using it to fuel four to eight hours of light at night. Solar lights can be used for flood lights, patio and deck lights, walkway or driveway lights, even for lights that illuminate your house number. Real Goods offers a number of good brands, from $80 to $400.

Decorate with light colors

Dark colors absorb light; light colors reflect it, reducing the need for artificial lighting. Light-colored paint, wall paper, carpeting, and drapes can go a long way towards brightening up your home and cutting energy needs.

IN THE KITCHEN

A look around your kitchen will show you that it's probably the most energy-hungry room in your house. If it's like most kitchens, it has at least a refrigerator, stove, and dishwasher, if not a microwave oven, toaster, coffee maker, blender, and television. This doesn't include several overhead and space lights. Appliances can account for 10% of your energy output, so use them efficiently and wisely.

Use manual instead of electrical appliances

We have become so completely dependent on the ease electricity affords that we have converted perfectly good manual appliances into electrical ones. Can openers, coffee grinders, beaters--just look around your kitchen and see how mechanized and energy-dependent it is. Pull some of those cords out of the electrical socket and start using a hand coffee grinder and a can opener with a hand twist. You'll save energy and participate more actively in preparing the food you eat. Don't stop there. Unhook yourself from electricity and gas as much as you can. Use clocks that you wind and lawn mowers whose blades are powered by your pushing.

Check an appliance's energy rating before you buy it

Manufacturers are required by law to place labels on major appliances showing how much it costs to operate them over a year's time. Look for the yellow and black label on the backside or bottom of an appliance and compare it with other models. For more information on buying energy-efficient appliances, consult "The Most Energy-Efficient Appliances," published by the Council for an Energy Efficient Economy. See below for ordering details.

Cooking

Boil liquids in a lidded pot

Don't ask me to remember the physics of this, but a pot of water boils faster when the top is on it.

Heat pots on the right-sized burner

On an electric stove, the whole burner coil heats up, so a lot of electricity is wasted around the edges when the coil is heating a pot smaller than itself. Likewise, a small coil will heat a big pot less efficiently than a bigger burner will.

Turn off electric burners or ovens before a job is done

Your oven or stove-top burner is still emitting heat after you've turned it off. That residual heat can be used to save energy. Turn off the burners a few minutes before the cooking time is up, and the residual heat will continue to cook. The same goes for the oven. But remember: this obviously applies only to electric burners. When gas burners are turned off, all the heat is off.

Use small appliances for small jobs

Use your oven to cook your turkey or a big dinner for a crowd, but if you're only cooking a single serving of macaroni and cheese or heating up a plate of leftovers, use your toaster oven or microwave. (Surprisingly, microwave ovens are generally more energy-efficient than regular ovens). You'll use less energy and cook your food faster.

Use the oven for multiple jobs

Plan out your baking so that you cook a number of dishes at the same time. If you've got three or four dishes that need to cook at different temperatures, select the average of the temperatures and cook all the dishes together. Of course, this is easier to pull off if the separate temperatures aren't radically different. If it's not possible, consider cooking one of the dishes in the microwave or toaster oven.

Don't open the oven door

Every time you open the oven door the temperature automatically drops between 25 to 75 degrees. If you're a chronic peeker, get an oven door with a glass window.

Make a solar box cooker

This cardboard box is the most energy-efficient "stove" you'll find. The cooker is made up of a cardboard box placed inside a bigger, insulated one. On top of the box is a glass lid and at one edge is an adjustable solar reflector, which, when raised, directs sunlight through the glass and into the box. The bottom of the box is painted black and absorbs heat, raising the temperature of the "oven". On sunny days the oven can get as hot as 275 degrees. And even though the oven is made from combustable materials, it won't catch fire. Easy-to-cook foods, such as eggs and chicken, take 1 to 2 hours; breads, potatoes, and most meats take 3 to 4 hours. All you need is cardboard, a pane of glass, aluminum foil, a black metal tray, some glue, and crumpled newspaper. For complete directions send $5 to Solar Box Cookers International, 1724 11th Street, Sacramento, CA 95814; 916-444-6616. They'll send you complete directions and great "solar" recipes.

Dishwashing

Do small dish loads by hand

The average dishwasher uses 14 gallons of water per load, but you can do small loads by hand with only 10 gallons. You use less water and less energy. It's close, but dishwashers can probably do bigger loads more efficiently. See the Water Conservation chapter for details.

Fill up your dishwasher

If you use a dishwasher, fill it up. Full loads use the same amount of water and energy as small loads, so make sure the resources are put to their fullest use.

Don't use the dishwasher's drying cycle

During the drying cycle, heat is pumped into the dishwasher to dry dishes quickly. Open your dishwasher before the drying cycle and let your dishes air dry.

Scrape your dishes

Debris from your dishes can accumulate and damage your machine. Scrape them before loading them in, but don't rinse them if not absolutely necessary. If you have to rinse, use cold water.

Refrigerating

Don't put hot foods into the refrigerator right away

The heat generated from a plate of hot food raises the temperature inside the refrigerator, forcing the thermostat to kick on. Let your food cool down for 15 or 20 minutes before putting it in the fridge.

Regulate your refrigerator's temperature

Unless your milk freezes, you probably haven't thought much about the temperature in your refrigerator. But there's a good chance it's too cold, and thus using up more energy than it needs to keep your perishables cold. The recommended temperature is 38 degrees for the fridge, 5 degrees for the freezer. You can't tell how cold your fridge is by looking at the thermostat, so place a thermometer inside it for a few hours and see how cold it gets. If it's not within a degree or two of the recommended temp, keep adjusting your thermostat and measuring the temperature until you get it right.

Don't open up fridge and freezer doors frequently

Appliances on thermostats work most efficiently when their environments are stable; opening the refrigerator door, even for a few seconds, alters that environment and forces the machine to replace the lost cool air. You can usually hear the generator click on soon after you've opened the door. Constantly opening and closing the door will keep your fridge in high gear as it tries to reach that constant temperature and sustain it. And since the average American opens the refrigerator 22 times a day, your fridge is constantly working overtime. So, think about the things you want from the refrigerator before you open the door, and get them all in one trip.

Keep your fridge well-maintained

This means dusting off the condenser coils on the back or bottom of the refrigerator and making sure the condensate drain (on self-defrosting units) is clear. You could be losing a lot of cold air due to worn seals around the door. To check, put a piece of paper between the seal and the metal cabinet. If there is no resistance when you pull it out, you probably need a new seal. Try all sections of the door.

Buy a Sunfrost refrigerator/freezer

The people who built the Sunfrost refrigerator knew a thing or two about energy efficiency. They mounted the compressor and condenser on top of the unit instead of on the bottom, so that the heat generated by these work horses escapes into the air instead of up into the cabinet itself. They also enveloped the interior in a thick layer of insulation. The Sunfrost uses only 350 watthours per day, compared to 3,000 for regular units. It costs a little more ($1,200 to $2,395), an investment you will quickly recoup in energy savings. It's available through Real Goods.

HOT WATER

Hidden away in a remote corner of your basement is the hardest working and most unappreciated of appliances: your hot water heater. Running day and night, it provides on demand instant hot water for showers, dishwashers, washing machines, and all your faucets. It takes a lot of energy to deliver that service; hot water heaters use up almost as much energy as your heating and air conditioning systems.

Use cold water whenever possible

You don't use any energy to get cold water. It's sitting in the treatment plant, ready to go. Use this energy-free alternative to hot water for washing clothes, rinsing dirty dishes, and doing cleaning chores.

Cut back on hot water use

For the times you use hot water, try to use less of it. You'll use half the hot water necessary for a bath if you take a short shower, and installing low-flow shower heads and faucet aerators can reduce by 60% the amount of hot water you go through. Also, repair leaky faucets. See the Water Conservation chapter for details.

Service your hot water tank

You can improve the performance of your hot water heater by adding insulation around the hot water pipes and by covering electric heaters with special insulating jackets.

Check your heater's water temperature. Your water heater's temperature gauge was set at the factory, and if your heater is like most, it was set to 140 degrees. If you don't have a dishwasher, you really only need the water to be 120 degrees. You can't determine by just looking at it which temperature your gage is set to, so draw off some water from the spigot at the bottom of the heater and measure it with a thermometer. Adjust the temperature gauge accordingly.

WORK WITH YOUR LOCAL UTILITY

After you've done an energy audit and have gotten a better idea of how you want to start conserving energy, call your utility company. There are over 1,300 energy efficiency programs across the country, sponsored by utility companies, which offer everything from free advice to rebates for using low-energy appliances. One utility company in Arizona credits customers $75 for adding reflective film to their windows, and the utility company servicing Osage, Iowa loans out a machine which measures an appliance's energy use. Other companies in Washington, California, and Wisconsin offer rebates to customers who buy low-energy household appliances. Call your utility company and see what assistance they can give you.

For more information

Before you spend $40 for a new toaster or $200 for a new air conditioner, spend $3 for "The Most Energy-Efficient Appliances." Published by the Council for an Energy Efficient Economy, the booklet will guide you in selecting the best brand for your money. ACEEE's "Saving Energy and

Money with Home Appliances" is also worth another $3 investment. Contact: American Council for an Energy Efficient Economy, 1001 Connecticut Avenue, NW, Suite 535, Washington, DC 20036; 202-429-8873.

The Department of Energy's "Tips for Energy Savers" also offers scores of ways to save energy. It's free for the writing. Contact: U.S. Department of Energy, Editorial Services, Office of Public Affairs, Washington, DC 20585; 202-586-5000.

For a toll-free phone call you can find out anything you need to know about how to conserve energy. The National Appropriate Technology Assistance Service (NATAS), which is sponsored by the U.S. Department of Energy, employs a staff of specialists to answer consumer questions on any aspect of energy conservation. An operator takes your question over the phone and refers it to a specialist, who answers your query within two weeks, either by phone or mail. The service is free. For more information, contact: NATAS, P.O. Box 2525, Butte, MT 59702-2525; 1-800-428-2525; in Montana: 1-800-428-1718.

part two

getting more involved

"Although I lived in Girgaum, I hardly ever took a carriage or a tram car. I had made it a rule to walk to the high court. It took me quite forty-five minutes and of course I invariably returned home on foot."

Mahondas Gandhi

CHAPTER 7

TRANSPORTATION
TREADING LIGHTLY ON THE EARTH

It's pretty well agreed that from an environmental perspective, the automobile is the worst way to travel. Cars are the biggest producers of carbon dioxide, the gas which most contributes to the greenhouse effect, and they spew into the air over 7 million tons of nitrogen oxide, which later falls back to earth as acid rain. Valuable resources are depleted to manufacture cars, and even more are used·to keep them running. Of all the oil our country uses, 63% percent goes to fueling motor vehicles; cars alone on any single day consume 82 million gallons of gas.

This is just at the end of the cycle. The environment takes a beating at every juncture of the infrastructure that's set up to support automobiles. In the last 20 years, over half a billion gallons of crude oil and fuel have spilled into our oceans and waterways, killing untold numbers of fish and wildlife and forever altering natural cycles. Over thirty-eight million acres of once wild land have been paved over for roads and parking spaces, equaling the state of Georgia in size. The process by which cars are manufactured spews additional sulphur and nitrogen into the air, and valuable land is used as a dumping ground for discarded automobiles, where battery acid leaches into the groundwater and burning tires send up black plumes of pollution. And all this for a vehicle to transport us quickly from one place to another. Clearly, it's a toll we can no longer afford to pay.

Walk

You'll walk down to the end of the street to mail a letter or around the corner to visit a friend. But what's your limit? How far away does a destination have to be before you drive instead of walk? One street over? Two blocks? A mile? To learn your limit, think of specific places you visit frequently--the convenience store, a restaurant, the dry cleaners--and determine how far away they are and how you normally get there. If you're like most people, you hop into your car to go just a few blocks.

Now, seriously consider walking there instead of driving. I'm not talking about going across town, but I do mean extending your limit. A walk to the convenience store that's a mile round trip is not that far. It's better for your health, the environment, and your peace of mind. It forces you to slow down and observe things that are never seen by a driver. Choose different streets every time you walk and look at the houses, greet the people, watch the seasons change, and become part of your neighborhood. You'll find that walking is more than just a means of transporting yourself from place to place, it's a state of mind.

Ride a bicycle

Chances are you have a bicycle; odds are that it spends most of its time on its kickstand in the garage. When you do use it, it's usually for exercise or recreation, riding around the neighborhood on a sunny Sunday afternoon. But your bike can also take care of a lot of your transportation needs. Leave your *car* in the garage and ride your bike to work. If you have to carry your bike a ways once you get to work (or need to bring it onto a train or bus), you can buy a bike that folds up. When you go shopping, attach a basket to the front handle bars or the back frame and cart your groceries back from the grocery store. Use it to go to the drug store, the library, or for any errand.

In addition to getting some exercise and taking a load off the environment, you'll save a lot of money. One study found that if commuters rode bikes to work, each one would save 150 gallons of gas a year. That's just for commuting. Think of all the gas you use for short trips and errands that can be saved by biking, to say nothing of the money you'll save on health club fees.

There is, on average, one bicycle for every two people in the United States. But despite such a large number of bikes, we haven't done a very good job at making riding convenient. Roads, as any biking commuter will tell you, were built for cars, and cars are not accommodating when it comes to sharing the road with their slower, pedaling counterparts. If you live in the city, biking downtown in rush-hour traffic on regular roads can be difficult and dangerous. More biker-friendly cities, like Seattle, are beginning to construct bikers' lanes, but in most areas, bikers' rights are a low priority. If you want to get involved in encouraging bicycling as a viable form of transportation, contact the following organizations: Bicycle Federation of America, 1818 R Street, NW, Washington, DC 20009, 202-332-6986; League of American Wheelmen, 6707 Whitstone Road, Suite 209, Baltimore, MD 21207, 301-944-3399; Bicycle Network, P.O. Box 8194, Philadelphia, PA 19101; Transportation Alternatives, 270 Lafayette, New York, NY; 212-941-4600.

Use skates

A new breed of rider has joined the bikers, walkers, and joggers on the bikepath these days. She's wearing a pair of roller skates or roller blades, and she's blowing by you at a good clip. But skaters aren't just on bikepaths. More and more, I see them on the streets and sidewalks, carrying parcels, and yes, going to work. Kids skateboard to each others' homes. It's great exercise, fast, and, as long as you bring along another pair of shoes to change into, convenient. It can be dangerous unless you know what you're doing, so learn how to use those rubber stoppers and stay off the busy streets.

Ride scooters and motorcycles

If your destination is just too far to walk or bike to, use a moped or motorcycle. Since they don't have to lug a multi-ton chassis around, they are faster and more fuel-efficient than cars. They are especially good if you live in a city and work downtown. You can take back streets to avoid traffic, and parking is usually easier. Chain them up well though, motorcycles and mopeds have high theft rates.

Use public transportation

Public transportation has an ill-deserved reputation as being second-class transportation. Ask people what they think of it and they will tell you about smells, overcrowding, uncomfortable chairs, bumpy rides, and long waits at bus stops in miserable weather. Of course, most of them haven't actually used public transportation themselves in a while, but try getting them on a crosstown bus to change their minds.

Granted, public transportation is not as convenient or comfortable as your car. And there may be times when you'll wait a while at a bus stop in bad weather or have to stand in a crowded train. But public transportation has made real gains in the last few years, and in many places it is an enjoyable and convenient way to get around. In Chicago, there are more than four buses for every thousand people and almost everyone lives within a five-minute walk of a bus stop or train station. Most trains and half of all the buses run 24 hours a day; you can get to any part of the city for less than $2. There are equally good systems in cities such as Atlanta, the District of Columbia, Seattle, and San Francisco.

The benefits of using public transportation? You don't have to deal with the aggravation of traffic or finding and paying for a parking spot. You'll spew fewer toxics into the air, and save money on gas, parking, and wear and tear on your car. You'll have time to read the morning paper or a novel, or catch up on some sleep. Call the local transit authority for information on your public transportation system.

Carpool

If you have to use your car, then increase its efficiency by putting more people in it. Carpooling can be especially convenient for commuters who work in the same office or in the same part of town. Some cities, such as Miami, reward commuters by giving them special lanes to make their trip faster. If passengers kick in a couple of bucks a week for gas and share driving duties, they can save a lot of money, get to know their fellow workers better, and greatly reduce the amount of air pollution. If you're interested in starting a carpool, talk to your company's human resources department. It may be able to put you in touch with other employees who carpool or help you set up a group. Alza, a pharmaceutical company in California, runs a public transportation program that subsidizes gas cost for carpoolers. Encourage your company to set up a similar program. To start your own carpool, talk to your co-workers and post messages on the company bulletin board.

Drive a car--efficiently

If you drive a car, there are things you can do to lessen its impact on the environment. Begin with your driving habits. Gunning the engine at green lights and stopping quickly at red lights and stop signs robs your car of energy for no real use. Coast to a stop and slowly give your car gas to get it going again. Drive steadily and try to avoid stop and start traffic. When you're on the open road, drive at 55 mph; you won't get to your destination as soon as you would by driving at 70 mph, but at 55 mph you'll save gas--over 15%--and your car will burn what you have more efficiently. To take even more strain off your car, remove any heavy, excess baggage from the trunk or back seat. For each additional hundred pounds in the car, your fuel economy drops one percent.

Planning can also increase your car's efficiency. Consolidate trips to the grocery store, shopping center, restaurants. If you need to go out and buy groceries, do it in the same trip that you drop your child off at baseball practice. Or do it on the way home from work. If you have no other reason to go out and you don't need the groceries right away, wait to do it until you have another errand to run. When you go on extended trips, use the shortest route. Better yet, take a train or bus if you can.

Buy a fuel-efficient car

If you have to buy a car, buy one that gets the best gas mileage. Improving your gas mileage, more than anything else you can do to increase your car's efficiency, will reduce the amount of carbon dioxide it emits. This usually means getting a small, lightweight car, but that doesn't necessarily mean that it will be cramped or unsafe. Compact and subcompacts are roomier than ever before, and they have been redesigned and made with different materials so that many are actually safer than their heavy-duty counterparts. And when looking around, remember that all those amenities, such as power steering, automatic transmission, and air conditioning, significantly decrease your gas mileage.

Modern fuel-efficient cars are not like their tin-can prototypes of the 70s. Just look at the Hondas and Toyotos. And it's not just the Japanese who are producing them. The

Ford Festiva, an American make, is one of the most fuel-efficient cars available in this country. To find out which cars have the highest fuel economy, consult the EPA's "Gas Mileage Guide." You can get them at auto showrooms or direct from the EPA. Contact your local EPA branch or the Washington headquarters at 401 M Street, SW, Washington, DC 20460; 202-382-2090. Here's a sampling from that list (all models are manuals):

SUBCOMPACTS	mpg city	mpg highway
Geo Metro XFI	53	58
Suzuki Swift	40	50
Daihatsu Charade	38	42
Ford Festiva	35	41
Honda Civic	33	37
COMPACTS		
Ford Escort	32	42
Isuzu Stylus	32	37
Pontiac Lemans	31	40
SMALL STATION WAGONS		
Honda Civic	31	34
Plymouth Colt	28	34
Dodge Colt Vista	28	34

Maintain your car

Your car may not be able to get the gas mileage of the Geo Metro, but there are ways of greatly improving its efficiency. Most of this advice has to do with maintenance: take care of your car and it will run better for you. The most obvious place to start is with a tune up every 5,000 to 10,000 miles. An engine that's out of tune could be using up 3% to 9% more gas than it should. Fuel efficiency is also improved by using a high-grade motor oil, such as 10W-30 and 10W-40, and by changing the air filter.

Keep an eye on your tires. When underinflated they flatten out more on the road, causing greater drag and making your car's engine work harder. The result: you use up 10% more gas. And since the tread's grip on the road is uneven, the tires wear out much faster; a tire that's underinflated by 15% loses 10% of its tread life. Radial tires improve fuel efficiency because of their built-in steel bands, which help keep tires from flattening out. Properly inflated, they can improve gas mileage by 3% to 7%, more for highway travel. Check the side of your tire for the recommended PSI.

Buy a solar car

Solar-powered vehicles are not a thing of the future anymore; they are here and you can buy one. In Switzerland, over a thousand legally-registered solarmobiles are driving the streets, soaking up free and non-polluting energy from the sun. Using some 6 kilowatthours of electricity, they can go about sixty miles at a 40 mph clip. Not enough to compete with regular automobiles, for sure, but solar drivers must have some satisfaction in their clean transportation when carbon dioxide-producing cars zip by. You can get a solarmobile for around $10,000. Tour de Sol will send you a list of the various solar vehicles for sale in Switzerland. Contact: Tour de Sol, Postfach 73, 3000 Bern 9, Switzerland. If you want to build one yourself, Suntools will give you everything you need to construct the Vanda, a two-seat solarmobile. The kit costs about $7,000. For more information contact: Suntools, 271 Franklin Avenue, Willitis, CA 95490; 707-459-2453.

Separate yourself from your car

Stop thinking of your car as an extension of your personality or as an indicator of your self-worth. These are ideas that have been drilled into us by car manufacturers and advertisers who are interested solely in making a profit. Can you manage with a less elaborate model? Can you do without a car at all? These are the questions we must force ourselves to consider.

"A land ethic changes the role of Homo sapiens from conqueror of the land-community to plain member and citizen of it. It implies respect for his fellow-members, and also respect for the community as such."

Aldo Leopold, *The Land Ethic*

CHAPTER 8

PROTECTING ANIMALS
RESPECTING THE RIGHTS OF FELLOW CREATURES

Tell someone that humans are *just* animals and he will probably tell you how we are *more* than animals, how our intelligence, spiritual nature, and advanced evolution have separated us from other, lower forms of life. He might even tell you that these very qualities have enabled humans to subdue animals, an ability which further proves just how different we are from them.

There are differences between man and other animals, of course, although not as great as we would like to think (just look at a man devouring a piece of fried chicken with his hands). But our emphasis on differences has too often been used as a way of denying the bond that exists between us and our four-legged counterparts. And the denial of this bond has allowed us to further deny our responsibility to protect and care for them. Lacking that sense of responsibility, we have been able with a free conscience to slaughter creatures for any purpose that has suited us--for food, clothing, or just for fun. We've done it so well that we've killed off entire species and pushed thousands more to the brink of extinction. When we're not directly shooting them, we're forcing them from their homelands or destroying and polluting the natural environment in which they live and upon which they depend for survival.

But whether or not we recognize it, we *are* animals and we are part of a larger community. We are also learning, slowly and perhaps too late, that our actions as they affect the wild community, eventually affect us. Whole ecosystems are already being drastically altered due to the extinction of native animals, and as these systems change, they

will alter natural cycles around the globe. These changes
will affect the environment we live in, our homelands.
Eventually, the slaughter of our fellow creatures will come
back to haunt us long after the animals are gone. We are
animals all right, just not very smart ones.

Don't buy products made from endangered or threatened animals

Open up your wardrobe and look at the clothes and acces-
sories inside. In all likelihood, some, if not many, are made
from the pelts and skins of animals: a leather jacket; a
snakeskin belt; a coat make from the pelts of foxes, racoons,
rabbits, or minks; crocodile skin boots; shoes or a purse
made from alligator skins. Go over to your dresser and
look in your jewelry box. Inside there may be a piece of
jewelry made from the ivory of an elephant's tusk--a
bracelet, necklace, or carved pendant. You might also have
a bracelet, ring, or eyeglass frames made from tortoise or
turtle shells; maybe even a snake or eel skin wallet. Have
you ever thought about what it is to wear the body part of an
animal that was killed for your adornment, especially considering that there are perfectly good non-animal substitutes?

The problem has greater consequences when the product is
made from an endangered or threatened animal. First, it's a
crime to buy items made from animals that are protected. The
list of items is long, but it includes many reptile skins and
leathers (from most crocodiles, lizards, snakes, and turtles),
birds and feathers (many exotic birds, especially certain par-
rots, macaws and cockatoos, and their feathers), ivory from
elephant tusks, and certain furs (from jaguars, leopards,
tigers, ocelots, seals, polar bears, and others). You'll lose your
purchase (and the money you paid for it) if it's found to have
come from an endangered animal.

More importantly, though, when you buy a product made
from an endangered animal, knowingly or not, you support its extinction. As long as there is a market for ivory
and fur pelts, poachers will continue to slaughter
elephants and walruses, and deplete the population of
wild tigers and leopards. Wearing an imitation is just as
bad. An animal may not have been killed, but your wearing an imitation sustains general interest in the fashion and
encourages less knowledgeable consumers to buy the real
thing. The same holds for real pelts and skins that are given
to you as gifts.

To learn more about endangered species, contact the U.S. Fish and Wildlife Service, Division of Endangered Species, P.O. Box 3247, Arlington, VA 22203; 202-343-3245. The World Wildlife Fund also publishes "Buyer Beware," a free brochure on the importation of illegal wildlife products. Contact WWF, 1250 24th Street, NW, Washington, DC 20037; 202-293-4800.

Report poaching

If you're in a park or other wildlife area and see either hunters killing protected animals or evidence that they have done so, report it to the park director. You can also call the Poaching Hotline, a toll-free number supported by the National Parks and Conservation Association. The number is 1-800-448-NPCA. The National Wildlife Association will even offer you a reward if your information leads to the conviction of anyone killing a bald eagle in the United States. Contact the National Wildlife Federation, Bald Eagle Reward Program, 1400 16th St., NW, Washington, DC 20036; 202-797-6850.

Adopt an animal

In response to the possible extinction of certain animals, environmental "adoption agencies" have sprung up around the country, offering members the opportunity to support ongoing efforts to protect their group's animal. Whales, birds, deer, horses, and burros are among the animals available for adoption. The programs vary somewhat, but they essentially follow the same format: for anywhere from $10 to $300, you can "adopt" a specific animal. There's no adoption center to visit, per se, and you don't actually get to keep the animal and take it home. You select a particular whale or type of bird from a catalogue and send in your check, for which you get a photograph of "your" animal, an adoption certificate, and a newsletter which updates you on your animal group's progress. The majority of the check goes to supporting the organization's efforts to protect and preserve its animal.

The exception to this is the Bureau of Land Management's Adopt-a-Horse program. When you "adopt" a horse (or burro) you actually buy it and take it home. There's a probation period of a year to make sure you are properly caring for your animal, but after the time is up, the animal becomes yours for good.

Some of this may sound a little hokey, especially since there are other major environmental groups already devoted to helping these animals. The concept of adoption is essentially a marketing ploy, making the process of helping more personal. But the work that results is just as valuable as that of other groups. The money from adoptions goes to protection of the animal, and these animals on the edge of extinction need all the support they can get. And it's likely that you would be more interested in peregrine falcons after investing money to help one. You'd be even more interested in its fate when, as happens in Project Wind Seine, you received a note telling you where your falcon was recovered and how it has fared since its tagging. For more information about adoption programs, contact any of the following groups:

Whale Adoption Project
320 Gifford Street
Falmouth, MA 02540
508-564-9980

A project of the International Wildlife Coalition, the Whale Adoption project offers adopters over 65 individual whales to choose from. A brochure, complete with pictures, gives you the history and personality profile of each whale. Your money goes to IWC's research and preservation efforts, as well as to Greenpeace's whale-saving campaigns. You receive an adoption certificate, a photograph of "your" whale, a whale migration map, and a newsletter. Adoption is $15.

Project: Wind Seine
Cape May Bird Observatory
P.O. Box 3
Cape May Point, NJ 08212
609-884-2736

Cape May Bird Observatory captures and bands birds landing at the Cape in order to research the needs of migratory birds. Your money funds these research efforts. There are 27 types of birds for your selection, from white-throated sparrows to peregrine falcons. You receive an adoption certificate and information about your bird's recapture. Adoption ranges in price from $10 to $150.

Delaware Valley Raptor Center
RD #2, Box 9335
Milford, PA 18337
717-296-6025

The Center organizes the adoption of eagles, hawks, owls, and other "birds of prey". Your money is used for the treatment and rehabilitation of ill, injured, and orphaned birds. It also funds the cost of caring for unreleasable birds, which become "foster parents" to orphaned birds. You receive an adoption certificate, photograph of "your" bird, information sheet, decal, and newsletter. Adoption is from $15 to $60.

Adopt-A-Deer
Department of Wildlife Ecology
University of Wisconsin
Madison, WI 53706
608-263-6271

Through this University of Wisconsin program, you can adopt a deer and help fund research of deer migration. Your money goes to trap, tag, and follow the deer population of Northern Wisconsin. You get a report every two months, as well as a migration map and adoption certificate. The cost is $300 per deer, but you can "co-adopt" a deer for $100.

Adopt-A-Horse Program
U.S. Department of the Interior
Bureau of Land Management
350 S. Pickett Street
Alexandria, VA 22304
202-343-9435

This government program arranges for the adoption of excess wild horses and burros captured by the BLM. The animals are for sale; buyers take them home from centers around the country. You must prove you have the facilities to care for them and pass a year trial period before you're granted a full certificate of title. The limit is 4 animals per year. Adoption costs are $125 for a horse, $75 for a burro.

Volunteer at animal protection groups

Animal protection organizations are typically understaffed and underfunded, and rely heavily on the unpaid efforts of volunteers to carry out their work. There are hundreds of groups out there that need volunteers to do everything from helping raise and care for baby bald eagles, to studying the behavioral patterns of loons, to restocking streams with trout. Volunteering is a unique way to personally contribute to the effort to protect animals, and at the same time, to learn more about them.

Contact environmental organizations, parks and wildlife sanctuaries, universities, zoos, and even government agencies in your area for information. The "Connections" feature in *Buzzworm* magazine is a good place to learn about environmental jobs and volunteer opportunities. Also, Earthwatch, a non-profit group, supports environmental research by matching up scientists with volunteers who pay to go on field trips, and who thus contribute both physically and monetarily. There are scores of opportunities to work on animal protection projects. Contact: Earthwatch, 680 Mt. Auburn Street, Box 403, Watertown, MA 02172; 617-926-8200.

Boycott tuna fish

Tuna boats kill thousands of dolphins every year. The modern way to catch tuna is for boats to throw into the ocean big nylon nets, which drag the water behind the boats and scoop up whatever tuna is in their path. This method, called driftnetting, can catch a lot of tuna, especially considering that the nets are up to 50' long and 40 miles wide. But besides somehow seeming an unfair way to fish for tuna, driftnetting also kills all other sea creatures caught within the net's expanse. Every year hundreds of thousands of dolphins, porpoises, seals, birds, sea turtles, and even whales are caught in driftnets and drowned. Dolphins are especially hard hit by the method, because fishermen hunt for them to locate tuna (tuna, for some reason, can often be found swimming underneath herds of dolphins). Helicopters and speedboats herd the dolphin, and thus the tuna below them, into groups, while fishermen throw their nets into the water and troll for the catch. The dolphins, caught in nets that are dragged for up to 12 hours before being pulled up, are unable to surface for air, and drown. More than 100,000 dolphins die this way every year. And their deaths are completely senseless; there are few commercial uses for dolphin, so their bodies are thrown overboard after being hauled up and picked out of the nets.

The biggest offenders of driftnet fishing are Japan, South Korea, and Taiwan. Laws restrict driftnetting aboard U.S. vessels. But to circumvent the restriction, a number of U.S. tuna companies have set up subsidiaries overseas and have begun buying tuna from foreign vessels not subject to American laws. There is also evidence which indicates that tuna fishermen still working in the United States have either hindered or bribed officials from documenting the number of dolphin killed per catch.

In response to the continued widespread killing of dolphin and other sea animals through driftnetting, the Earth Island Institute in 1988 initiated a boycott of all canned tuna. The targeted tuna companies include H.J. Heinz (makers of Star-Kist) and Ralston Purina (Chicken of the Sea), the largest processors of tuna in the United States. Keep their products, especially their tuna fish, out of your cupboards, and swallow your craving for a tuna fish sandwich. You might just save a dolphin. For more information on the tuna boycott, contact Earth Island Institute, 300 Broadway, Suite 28, San Francisco, CA 94133; 415-788-3666.

Cut up six-pack rings

Once it's in the water, the plastic ring that holds together your six-pack of beer, cola, or fruit juice is a floating noose. Invisible to fish, seals, and birds swooping down into the water for a catch, that loop can easily slip around an animal's neck or snout, causing it to suffocate, drown, or starve to death.

These rings make it into the water from boaters throwing trash overboard, sun bathers leaving garbage on the beach, and landfills from which trash is carried into nearby waters. The obvious answer is to keep the rings--and any trash--out of the water; but to be sure that your six-pack loops never end up around a bird's neck, snip them with scissors before you throw them away. This is true even if you live hundreds of miles from a major body of water. Much of our trash is trucked across the country, and it's hard to know just what landfill it ends up in. If you've seen a picture of a seal that's been strangled on a plastic loop, you'll want to be absolutely sure that noose didn't come from your kitchen.

Build a backyard wildlife habitat

Your own backyard can be a refuge for the animals in your area. Birds will nest in your trees and drink and clean themselves in your birdbath; bushes will attract visiting rabbits. The National Wildlife Federation can help you landscape your yard to encourage animal visitors. They'll send you everything you need to know about providing food, water, cover, and reproductive areas in your yard for wildlife. If you have a plan in mind yourself, draw it out and send it to NWF. For $5 they will review your design and make suggestions for improvement. For more information, contact Backyard Wildlife Habitat Program, National Wildlife Federation, 1400 16th Street, NW, Washington, DC 20036; 703-790-4000.

"He that plants trees loves others besides himself."

Thomas Fuller

CHAPTER 9

PLANTING TREES
HEALING THE ENVIRONMENT AND REGAINING A HERITAGE

There was a time when dense virgin forests covered the entire eastern region of the United States. White oaks, sugar and red maples, American elms and sycamores, bald cypresses, and longleaf pines stretched unimpeded from the tip of Maine to the Everglades of Florida, extending as far west as central Texas and up to Minnesota. Large stands in the West began at the Rockies, boasting the tallest and largest trees in the country. Douglas firs and giant sequoias towered over two hundred feet into the air, with circumferences so broad that thirteen men with arms outstretched could barely encircle one. But by 1850, nearly a quarter of these virgin forests had disappeared, and by the end of World War II, they were reduced to thin parcels of trees dotting the land. Today, the term "virgin forests" is almost an anachronism, and the logging of the remaining old growth stands, such as those in the Pacific Northwest, is well underway.

The disappearance of trees from our landscape is a loss of a large part of our heritage, but it has even more serious consequences for the environment. A treeless landscape contributes to soil erosion, the silting of rivers, crop losses, and rising temperatures. We are finding that trees are instrumental in maintaining a delicate balance of nature. They play a role in slowing the greenhouse effect by absorbing carbon dioxide that would otherwise reach the atmosphere and trap heat. Trees are even more effective at combatting global warming at it source--the burning of fossil fuels for energy. Shade trees can lessen the need for air conditioning by reducing room temperatures in the summer months by 20 degrees; trees planted as windbreakers can help keep homes warm in winter time, reducing heating bills by as much as 30%. Planting a tree is a simple act that can help lessen many environmental

problems, and it's one whose benefits will continue long
after we set the tree into the ground.

Plant a tree

Before you put that maple sapling in the ground, think
about your purpose for planting a tree. Do you want trees
that will bear fruit for homemade apple pies or are you
interested in cutting heating and air conditioning bills with
shade and windbreaking trees? Look around your yard,
street, or neighborhood plot and determine how best to
place the trees, considering such things as how many you
want to plant, how big they will grow, and whether there
are any potential obstacles, such as overhead utility lines.
Windbreak trees, for instance, block wind for a distance 10
times the height of the tree. Oak trees should be planted at
least 25 feet away from the house.

Then do some investigative work. Call your local arboretum, horticultural society, or tree-planting society and
find out the best varieties to plant. Remember, only plant
trees that are indigenous to your area. They will grow
better and need less maintenance, and chances are they are
available at your local nursery. For $2, the National Arbor
Day Foundation will send you "The Tree Book," a booklet
identifying the major trees, and areas of the country to
which they are best suited. You can even order saplings
from them for $6 to $8, with discounts for members. The
group will also tell you everything you need to know
about picking out the best tree for your plot, getting it into
the ground and caring for it. Contact National Arbor Day
Foundation, 100 Arbor Avenue, Nebraska City, NE 68410.
For a list of places to buy tree seedlings through the mail,
see the service directory under "tree seeds" (page 136).

A word of warning: you may want to become your
community's Johnny Appleseed, but don't sow your tree
seeds on public or private land without first getting permission and securing permits. To find out who owns a
piece of property, call your county's tax assessor. If you
can't find a place to plant a tree, grow one in a pot on your
back porch or in your sun room. There are whole varieties
of dwarf fruit trees specially cultivated for small containers.

HOW TO PLANT A TREE

When you buy a tree, it is most likely to come wrapped in
burlap or paper. Cut away any wire or nylon string and

remove the wrapping. If the roots are not covered by a ball of dirt, soak them in water for six hours. Dig a hole deep and wide enough so that the roots can spread out (tangled roots can eventually strangle a tree from underneath). Fill in the bottom half with dirt and pack firmly; add the rest of the soil and pack less firmly with your heel. Create a basin around the base to hold water. Soak. Add wood chips or gravel. Support trees thicker than 1 1/2 inches in diameter with stakes. Water well every week until the tree takes hold (usually for one to two years).

Join a tree-planting organization

If you'd rather not go it alone, hook up with one of the many tree-planting groups that have sprung up across the country. The most ambitious campaign, dubbed Global Releaf, has been launched by the American Forestry Association, which is looking to plant over 100 million trees by 1992. Most local organizations encourage the active participation of would-be tree planters, but they will also accept financial contributions from those looking more for spiritual than physical involvement. Contact the organization nearest you for more information.

TREE-PLANTING ORGANIZATIONS

Friends of Trees
P.O. Box 40851
Portland, OR 97240
503-233-8172

Global Releaf
American Forestry Association
P.O. Box 2000
Washington, DC 20013
202-667-3300

National Arbor Day Foundation
100 Arbor Avenue
Nebraska City, NE 68401
402-474-5655

Neighborwoods
Open Lands Project
220 S. State Street
Chicago, IL 60604
312-427-4256

Philadelphia Green
The Pennsylvania Horticultural Society
325 Walnut Street
Philadelphia, PA 19106
215-625-8250

Plant A Tree, Grow A Friend!
633 S. College
Ft. Collins, CO 80524
303-224-2877

Retree International
P.O. Box 346
Wilsonville, OR 97070

Tree People
12601 Mulholland Dr.
Beverly Hills, CA 90210
213-769-2663

Trees Atlanta
96 Poplar Street, NW
Atlanta, GA 30303
404-522-4097

Trees for Houston
P.O. Box 13096
Houston, TX 77219
713-523-8733

Trees for Life
1103 Jefferson
Wichita, KS 67203
316-263-7294

Spread the word with seed greeting cards

Before founding Ft. Collins' Plant A Tree, Grow A Friend!
organization, Scott Alyn was hard at work at his
brainchild, The Great Northwestern Greeting Seed Company, a company that produces greeting cards with seeds
in them. Alyn's "cards that grow" are a good way of
showing someone you care--about them and the earth. The
greeting cards contain vegetable and flower seeds, not tree
seeds, but they show that growing plants is a worthy and
important endeavor. Contact The Great Northwestern

Greeting Seed Company, P.O. Box 776, Oregon City, OR 97045; 503-631-3425.

Get more information

As part of its Paper Series, the Worldwatch Institute publishes "Reforesting the Earth," a brief look at deforestation. Single copies are $4; there are significant discounts for bulk orders. Contact the Worldwatch Institute, 1776 Massachusetts Avenue, NW, Washington, DC 20036; 202-452-1999.

If you are planning to start a tree-planting program in your community, you'll want to get the "Planting Project Workbook," a step-by-step guide to getting your community involved in planting. All aspects of tree planting are considered, including choosing a site, securing permits and permission, funding the project, and getting equipment and supplies. Send $12 to TreePeople, 12601 Mulholland Drive, Beverly Hills, CA 90210; 818-753-4600.

"We need to disrupt our own daily lives, and the lives of other folks, before those lives disrupt forever the planet."

Bill McKibben

CHAPTER 10

LOBBYING AND PROTESTING
VOICING YOUR OPINION

If you were a ruler and your town were your kingdom, no doubt you would change a few things. You'd close down the companies that spew pollution into the air from their smokestacks, deny permission to develop wooded areas, close down streets to automobiles, install streetcars and build bike lanes. Maybe you'd plant more trees and set aside land for neighborhood gardens. People would be happier and lead healthier, more fulfilling lives.

But you're not a ruler. You're part of a larger community, the members of which have a different vision of the way things should be. People want cars because cars transport them back and forth to work quickly; factories with smokestacks provide jobs; developed areas provide homes. You're not ruler, but you do have a say, especially when the reality of someone else's vision is damaging the earth and adversely affecting your life. You have a say when the pollution emitted from smokestacks increases the incidence of cancer in your community or when the development of wooded areas effects your town's water supply. It's times like those that call for you to voice your opinion and demand change. It's your right and your responsibility.

Keep abreast of what's happening in your neighborhood

There are countless stories of people waking up one morning, shocked to find big changes happening in their neighborhood. A wooded lot is razed to make room for a new housing complex, flight patterns at the nearby airport are switched to go directly overhead, a new chemical plant sets up shop on the edge of town. The changes have been in the works for months and the plans were approved by the county board and printed in the paper a long time ago. But these busy people never heard about it, and now it's too late to do anything to stop it. All because they thought someone else was keeping an eye out.

Decisions are made every day which affect your life. But you'll never know about them until it's too late to change them unless you start following the developments in your corner of the world. You can begin with reading the daily newspaper, especially the local section, as well as your neighborhood paper or newsletter. Watch the local news. Join your neighborhood's citizen group and attend city hall meetings. Pay close attention to the city's planning commission. It screens all new development that's planned for the area. Be vocal in the meetings; show the officials you're watching their moves, and remind them that you'll vote in the next election. Let them know that you're keeping an eye out.

Write to your congressperson

It's harder for you to address your concerns to your senator or representative as intimately as you can with your local representatives. They spend most of their time in Washington and have full agendas when they are in their home towns. But it's important that you let them know of your opinions. Congresspersons wield a lot of political power, and their votes will affect your life. If you are not sure who your representatives and senators are, consult the Congressional Directory at the end of this book.

Try to meet privately with your congressperson if possible; congresspersons are in their home offices periodically and during congressional recesses. But don't count on getting in to talk to them. They're pretty busy and can rarely spare the time for personal meetings with a voter ready to push a special interest on them. You may stand a better chance of getting in the door if you are with a group, but the odds are still against you.

This leaves you with a less personal, but potentially more useful form of communication--a letter. There's never been a survey of how effective letters have been in influencing an official to vote a certain way, but there are enough examples to suggest that letters can and do make a difference. The National Wildlife Federation, for instance, claims that the flood of letters pouring in to senators and representatives helped win support for the passage of the 1988 Endangered Species Act. Representative Morris Udall, one of the most influential environmentalists in office today, says he reads every letter sent to him and that on numerous occasions a letter influenced his thinking. Remember, congresspersons are just like any other elected officials; they may seem more remote and important, but they are still only in office because of your vote. So write your letter and be heard.

HOW TO WRITE A LETTER TO YOUR CONGRESSPERSON

Representative Udall, who knows more about getting letters from constituents than I do, wrote an article on how to write a good one, and I'm drawing on his information here. For Representative Udall, the important points are:

1) **Address the letter correctly.** Get the name and title right, and make sure it's sent to the correct address. Senators and representatives are both referred to as Honorable ("The Hon. Paul Simon") on the address. You greet senators with "Dear Mr. Senator" or "Dear Mr. Simon". Representatives, as befitting their lower salary, I guess, can't be greeted by their office, only by their last name ("Dear Ms. Schroeder"). The mailing address of senators is United States Senate, Washington, DC 20510; representatives are at United States House of Representatives, Washington, DC 20515.

2) **Identify the bill or issue.** Put the specifics out there right away so the congressperson knows what you're talking about. Give the number of the bill. If you don't know it, call the Clerk of the House at 202-225-7000. And send the letter before the bill is up for vote so the congressperson can read your letter and have time to think about it.

3) **Send the letter to *your* congressperson.** A congressperson who doesn't represent your congressional district can't do a lot for you. First of all, your views don't matter much since they don't tell a congressperson what her own constituents think. Secondly, her hands are tied, due to congressional courtesy, which essentially means that she shouldn't stick her nose into her colleague's business.

4) **Be brief and to the point.** Write a good letter. Spend some time developing your argument before putting it down on paper; when you're ready to write it down, make it as clear and as short as possible. Remember, your congressperson gets hundreds of these letters and doesn't

have time to figure out what you mean. Elaborate only if
you have new information to impart, some expert
knowledge.

5) Don't browbeat. Don't verbally abuse or threaten the
person you're writing to. You've got the power of a vote,
but if you berate your congressperson, he won't take your
letter seriously and may write you off. Think how you
would react if you were in his position. Remember, the
purpose is to persuade, not to judge. And give him credit
if it's due.

6) Consider FAXing. If your letter isn't going to make it to
the congressperson's office in time if it goes by regular
mail, FAX it to her. Consult the Congressional Directory
for a listing of congressional FAX numbers.

Call your congressperson

Every year, more and more mail floods into the Postmaster
of the Office of the House, the center which processes
congressional mail. Last year, almost 400 million pieces of
mail were sent to members of congress, up almost 300%
from the previous year. There's no way a representative or
senator can sort through and carefully consider that
volume of mail. One representative, Frank Horton (R, NY)
claims that a phone call is the better way to go. You won't
be able to talk directly to your congressperson, but you can
briefly express your views to a staff person, who will add
them to tally sheets. A central office transfers calls to
individual senators and representatives. For senators call
202-224-6391 (Republican) or 202-224-8541 (Democrat); for
representatives call 202-225-7350 (Republican) or 202-225-
7330 (Democrat). Consult the Congressional Directory for
the direct phone number to a congressperson's office.

Follow the voting record of your congressperson

Keeping track of how your congressperson votes on environmental issues can be difficult. Votes on issues that
don't have much media interest won't get good coverage,
if any. Recognizing that, the League of Conservation
Voters has made it easy for you. This group closely
watches how each representative and senator votes on
environmental issues and prints the results in its *National
Environmental Scorecard*. Floor votes and sponsorship of
environmental legislation are both taken into account.
Congresspersons are then rated according to their overall
performance within the environmental arena. To get a

copy of the *Scorecard*, contact: League of Conservation Voters, 2000 L Street, NW, Washington, DC 20036; 202-785-8683.

Vote

Behind each phone call or letter to your representative or senator is the power of your vote, the implied threat that you will not re-elect that person if she doesn't support your view. If your congressperson continually votes against environmental legislation, make good on your threat and vote her out of office.

Protest

There are times when letters, phone calls, and established channels are just not enough. Sometimes it takes tough talk and tough action to show you mean business. You've got to protest. There are lots of ways to do this, everything from boycotting and picketing to participating in sit-ins or chaining yourself to the gates of a polluting factory. Think about the method that makes the most sense to you.

The easiest way is to join a protest movement that's already been formed. A crowd usually gets more attention than an individual, and more of the work can be divided among the members. Well-organized movements have brought down irresponsible companies and drawn national attention to the real problems of toxic pollution and environmental degradation. However, don't let that prevent you from forming your own movement or acting alone. You know what kind of environmental damage is going on in your neighborhood, and often, if you don't take charge no one will.

Tackling polluters is a big and extremely demanding job. Fortunately, there are a number of groups out there that can help you. Perhaps the best one is Citizen's Clearinghouse for Hazardous Wastes, a group that grew out of Lois Gibbs' protest movement at Love Canal. In addition to providing you with the scientific and technical assistance you'll need to understand toxic problems, CCHW can help you set up your protest movement and attract community involvement. For more information, see the directory of environmental organizations on page 121. Another good source is the Institute for Local Self-Reliance, which focuses on helping communities develop alternatives to environmentally unsound practices. Contact the Institute for Local Self-Reliance, 2425 18th Street, NW, Washington,

DC 20009; 202-232-4108. Also consult the local branch of a national environmental organization. They may be able to give you a lot of assistance.

If more radical forms of protest appeal to you, contact Greenpeace. The group has had almost 20 years of practice in perfecting protest movements, and they can help you rally your troops and get good media coverage. See the entry for Greenpeace on page 124. For those of you who are attracted to the direct actions of Earth First!, read Dave Foreman's *Ecodefense*. This illustrated guidebook will show you everything you need to know about monkeywrenching, including how to take down a bulldozer, keep trees from being cut down, and keep from getting caught. You can order the book through the *Earth First! Journal* (see page 111 for details).

Boycott environmentally unsound products and manufacturers

Refusing to buy a certain product can be the most effective way of forcing its manufacturer to mend its wicked ways. Boycotting is fast--it begins with your next trip to the store--and it hits a targeted company right where it matters the most: in the pocketbook. The more visible and effective the boycott, the more the company has to lose. In addition to the loss of revenue up front, a boycotted company stands to lose even more money over the long term due to a tarnished reputation, a loss of employee moral, and a drop in production, all of which were built up with a lot of time and effort. So, when a company sees that you aren't buying its products, it takes notice and reacts. And don't be intimidated by a company's size or reputation; remember, it's dependent on *you*; you're not dependent on it.

The most effective boycotts are ones supported by a large group; the loss of a lot of customers is the loss of a lot of money. Sign up with boycotting groups, but don't let that keep you from boycotting on your own. By refusing to buy tuna fish, you may only be denying Ralston Purina (the makers of Chicken of the Sea tuna) less than a couple of dollars a month, but you are denying them at least *some* money. Ralston Purina won't fold without your $5 a month and probably won't even change its practices, but even on the most minute level they will feel your disapproval. And you can live with integrity.

You can then increase your impact by following up with a letter to Ralston Purina explaining why you didn't buy its tuna and that you will continue not to do so until it stops supporting fishing methods that kill dolphins. Companies read letters of complaint! (Expect to get a very defensive reply). Increase your influence even more by informing your friends about your boycotting and getting them to join. Tee shirts, bumper stickers, and buttons will help spread the word.

The big problem with boycotting is that you need to know of a company's evil ways before you can boycott it. Media sources, which are often supported or controlled by these companies, may be reluctant to report the dirt on them. And companies keep a tight lid on their actions, especially those which might raise the public's ire. Fortunately, there are a number of sources out there to keep you informed. First, quite a few environmental publications report on the practices of companies as they affect the environment. *Earth First! Journal*, *Greenpeace Magazine*, and *Earth Island Journal* are especially good, and they provide you with names and addresses of corporate leaders to send letters of protest to. One small booklet, *Shopping for a Better World*, put out by the Council on Economic Priorities, rates companies according to their level of social responsibility. The book is easy to use and fits into your pocket. Send $5.95 to Council on Economic Priorities, 30 Irving Place, New York, NY 10003; 800-822-6435.

Two other publications deal exclusively with boycotting. *The National Boycott News* is a two hundred page magazine packed with information on the major boycotts which are in effect across the country. It will tell you everything you need to know about a boycotted company, including the reason for its boycott, the issues involved, the company's response, the group calling for the boycott, the company's products, and the names and addresses of people to write to. Contact the Institute for Consumer Responsibility, 6506 28th Avenue, NE, Seattle, WA 98115; 206-523-0421; subscriptions are $10 for four issues. Co-op America's fledgling *Action Boycott News* does the same thing on a less grand scale, but it may soon be upgraded. Contact Co-op America, 2100 M Street, NW, Suite 310, Washington, DC 20063; 800-872-5307. The publication is free for Co-op members; otherwise it's $1 an issue.

BUYcott

Boycotts ask people not to buy a certain product. A BUYcott, on the other hand, encourages consumers to buy products from companies that are very socially responsible. Ben & Jerry's Ice Cream should be the object of any ice-cream eater's BUYcott. Established to make money and make a contribution to the world at the same time, Ben & Jerry's has established itself as model of "corporate" responsibility. The company treats its employees well; the highest paid employee can earn only 5 times the salary of the lowest paid employee; employees get bonuses based on 5% of the profits; and there are trips to hockey and baseball games. Ben & Jerry's also donates time and money to charitable causes (over $300,000 to various organizations; free ice cream to fund-raising efforts), hires people with disabilities, and recycles (they feed local pigs with left-over milk solids). So, when you buy a product or service--any product or service--support the one which puts your money to uses you yourself would be proud of.

Support the Valdez Principles

Arising out of the disastrous Valdez oil spill in Alaska, the Valdez Principles are a set of guidelines which define what businesses must do to protect the environment. Among the points covered are cutting pollution, manufacturing safe products, conserving energy, and protecting employees' health. Co-op America, a non-profit organization providing environmentally-sound services, is leading this campaign that would encourage companies to follow the Principles. Those that agree to support them would be required to undergo an annual environmental audit, which would rate their impact on the environment. The audit would then become public.

Co-op America is busy with its public information campaign and needs your help. For more information, contact Co-op America, 2100 M Street, NW, Suite 310, Washington, DC 20063; 202-872-5307.

"We learn over and over with this movement that we have to develop strength. We have to develop the unity, the resources, the power within our own communities. It is when we unite with our neighbors that we win."

Penny Newman

CHAPTER 11

JOINING ENVIRONMENTAL ORGANIZATIONS
MEMBERSHIP IN THE MOVEMENT

Environmental organizations have been around for a long time, fighting for wilderness preservation, the protection of endangered species, and the right of nature to exist on its own terms. Since 1892, the Sierra Club has been actively preserving our wilderness heritage, keeping dams out of the Grand Canyon, getting land set aside for national parks, and playing a major role in establishing a national wilderness preservation system. The Audubon Society has just as strenuously protected birds and other wildlife since 1905, and for more than 50 years the Wilderness Society has pursued its mission to create and preserve wilderness areas.

But the public's involvement in these groups and in the environmental movement in general didn't really begin until the early 1970s, when the first Earth Day inspired people to do something about pollution. Hundreds of new environmental organizations sprang up across the country to meet the crisis head on, and flocks of converts signed up to become members. The movement got another big boost in the early 80s when James Watt became Secretary of the Interior and quickly began reversing hard-earned environmental gains. Almost overnight, horrified citizens swelled membership rolls in environmental organizations. Today, these organizations play an important role within the environmental movement, using the collective might of their memberships to fight for the preservation and protection of our wild places.

Get involved

Membership in an organization does more than just extend your personal political influence. Through publications and newsletters, organizations help keep you informed about the issues and the group's efforts to confront them. Some groups offer you opportunities to get intimately involved in planning and decision-making, while others encourage mass participation in the actual work of the club, be it preparing speeches given to neighborhood groups or planting trees and restoring wilderness areas. And participation in these groups can be fun. A number of groups sponsor wilderness hikes, camping trips, and extended outings in the wilds of foreign countries. But most of all, membership in groups can connect you with a larger community of concerned individuals who, like you, have the interests of the earth at heart.

HOW TO CHOOSE AN ORGANIZATION

So, you've got $25 and you want to join an environmental group. Now what? There are literally thousands of groups out there and it's tough to determine which one is most deserving of your support. Some names are familiar--the Sierra Club, Greenpeace, World Wildlife Fund--but you're not exactly sure what they do. You don't want to join just *any* group, but you don't have the time or resources at hand to fully research them all.

Yet you can still make an informed choice. To make the job easier, I have outlined a few things to consider in finding the group best suited to your interests and energy.

Determine the Issues you are interested in

All environmental organizations are involved in the fight to preserve and protect our wild places, but each group has its own agenda. Some groups narrow their focus to a particular issue or concern, such as nuclear energy or the tropical rainforests. The Citizen's Clearinghouse for Hazardous Wastes, for example, follows toxic pollution, and Ducks Unlimited looks to protect North America's waterfowl. Organizations like the Wilderness Society and Defenders of Wildlife have broader missions to preserve wild places and their inhabitants. Narrow your list down to the groups which pursue issues that are important to you.

Think about the methods a group uses to achieve its goals

Some organizations, like the Environmental Defense Fund, use litigation, while others look to educate the public and encourage citizens to exert political pressure. Recognizing that much of the fight for wilderness takes place in the political arena, most groups support lobbying efforts on Capitol Hill. But not all of them. The Nature Conservancy, for example, buys up land and tries to avoid the political machinations of Washington. Radical groups, such as Earth First!, are impatient with mainstream groups' willingness to compromise away pieces of wildlife, and so eschew the DC political scene. They adopt a hard-nosed attitude to preserving wilderness, which condones breaking the law when necessary. Do you feel that a person's chaining herself to a tree or disabling bulldozers is legitimate? How effective is compromise and the use of established political channels? Decide and commit accordingly.

Determine your level of involvement

Opportunities for personal involvement in The Wilderness Society, for example, are limited. Members receive periodic action alerts encouraging them to write to their elected officials, but they don't actively participate in the work of the Society. That's done by a paid staff, which is supported by your dues. The Sierra Club, on the other hand, encourages your involvement. Members can become active in local chapters, monitoring area concerns, assuming leadership roles within the organization, speaking before neighborhood groups, and taking part in hiking and backpacking outings. Think about how involved you want to be. And remember, it's O.K. to support an organization simply with your dollars.

DIRECTORY OF ENVIRONMENTAL ORGANIZATIONS

Starting on page 121 is a directory of environmental organizations. In that directory I have listed some of the better groups, with a brief description of their mission, as well as all the information you need to know to sign up with them. I have purposely kept the spectrum broad: conservative and radical, political and non-political, area-specific and general are mixed in here. There are also groups that just want your money, as well as those which also want your time (all groups need your money!). Read over the descriptions and see how they fit into your own interests. If you want more information on particular groups, call or write them. They will gladly send you an information packet.

A note: Environmental organizations are notorious for selling their mailing lists to one another, and you can be sure that once you're on one, your mailbox will soon be crammed full of solicitations from scores of organizations. So when you sign up with an organization, make sure you ask them *not* to put your name on its mailing list.

part three

going all the way

"Knowledge is of two kinds. We know a subject ourselves, or we know where we can find information upon it."

James Boswell, *Life of Johnson*

CHAPTER 12

ECO-EDUCATION
LEARNING MORE ABOUT RESPONSIBLE LIVING

Your interest in leading a more environmentally sound lifestyle will hopefully go beyond the reading of this book. *Embracing the Earth* is just a beginning, the first steps on how you can, as David Brower says, lessen your own burden on the earth. There's a lot more information out there and there are a number of sources worth consulting for the latest environmental news, environmentally sensitive products, and suggestions for living responsibly. This chapter shows you where to go to get that information.

Below I have listed the sources I have found to be among the most useful, everything from influential environmental publications to international computer networks. They are listed and described briefly, with all the information you need to gain access to them. The list is by no means exhaustive, and you don't need to consult them all. But if you consult even a few of them, you will gain a wealth of knowledge to help you further a commitment to responsible, and better, living. Good luck.

STATE OF THE WORLD: Understanding The Crisis

Every year Lester Brown and his colleagues at the Worldwatch Institute publish *State of the World*, an assessment of the world's condition from a global perspective. Environmental issues figure predominantly. The 1989 edition, written during the droughts and floods of 1988, devotes whole chapters to land degradation, ozone depletion, and grassroots activism, as well as shorter pieces to water shortages, air pollution, fuel efficiency, and toxic pollution. Besides being easy to read and to understand, the strength of the book rests in the comprehensiveness of its survey and the depth of its research. Instead of having to follow environmental issues by reading through a number of different publications, you can spend a few hours reading *State of the World* to get a good grasp on the major problems confronting the planet. The book is also strong in suggesting solutions to the environmental crisis. Most of the chapters examine possible answers; the final chapter in the 1989 edition outlines a global action plan.

To keep readers up to date on the issues between yearly publications of *State of the World*, the Worldwatch Institute also publishes periodic research booklets in its "Paper Series". The more than 90 papers available so far cover topics from hydropower to environmental refugees. In addition, the Institute puts out a bi-monthly magazine called *World Watch*, a shorter, magazine-style *State of the World*. As with the book, the magazine pieces are timely, informative, and easy to understand. The output of the Worldwatch Institute is a good indication that it takes seriously its mission to " change the course of history and help reverse the environmental trends that are undermining the human prospect." The organization is also independent and not-for-profit.

State of the World is available directly from Worldwatch in either hardcover ($18.95) or paperback ($9.95). If you wait a month or so after the book has been released, you can probably find a decent copy in a used book store. Worldwatch Papers are $4 each, with significant discounts for large orders. Subscription rates for *World Watch* magazine are $21. Contact Worldwatch Institute, 1776 Massachusetts Avenue, NW, Washington, DC 20036, 202-452-1999.

INFLUENTIAL ENVIRONMENTAL BOOKS: Putting It Into Perspective

In order for you to become knowledgeable in the environmental movement you will need a background in the basic issues. If you are interested in understanding the actions of Earth First!, for instance, it's helpful to know Ed Abbey's *The Monkeywrench Gang*, the novel that inspired the formation of the group. Likewise, the causes and consequences of the current agricultural crisis will be clearer after you read Wendell Berry's *Culture and Agriculture*, as will all the New Age talk about deep ecology and biocentrism after you finish Devall and Session's *Deep Ecology*. Gaining a fuller understanding of the major environmental issues will take some study, but to make the job easier, I have come up with a list of ten of the most important environmental works. The list is in no way exhaustive or objective, but each of the books mentioned has influenced the environmental movement in a particular way, and you will have a better picture of the range of issues involved after you read them.

With the exception of Bill McKibben's *The Death of Nature*, you should be able to find good second-hand copies of these books in used book stores. If you have trouble locating them or want new copies, I have listed the publishers of the most recent, and in most cases, the cheapest new editions.

THE ENVIRONMENTALISTS LIBRARY:
Ten of the most influential environmental books

Abbey, Ed. *The Monkeywrench Gang.* 1975.(Avon Books, 1976; Ballantine editons)

A soft-hearted general surgeon, an angry Vietnam vet, a relapsed Mormon with three wives, and a malcontented receptionist make up this entertaining novel written by the gadfly of the environmental movement. Abbey chronicles the adventures of this monkeywrench gang as they sabotage anything in their path that defiles, defaces, or destroys the environment. They burn billboards, decommission bulldozers, dynamite railroads, and knock out bridges, all in defense of the earth. Although wickedly funny, *The Monkeywrench Gang* takes a serious look at the purpose, techniques, and consequences of ecotage. The book is credited for inspiring the formation of the radical environmental group Earth First!, which Abbey himself supported.

Berry, Wendell. *The Unsettling of America: Culture and Agriculture.* 1977 (Sierra Club Books, 1986)

Written during Earl Butz's tenure as Secretary of Agriculture, *The Unsettling of America* decries the waste, greed, and irresponsibility of today's agribusiness, and argues for a more nurturing agriculture and more responsible living. A farmer himself, Berry is an outspoken advocate of the small farm, and here he establishes the philosophical foundation of his argument. The book critically examines the concepts of progress/growth, manufacturing/cultivating, stewardship, limitations, community, and health--tying them not just to farming but to our culture and character as well. The solutions Berry proposes to the

present agricultural crisis are just as insightful and urgent-
ly needed now as they were in the late 1970s.

Carson, Rachel. *Silent Spring*. 1962. (Many new editions)

This 1962 study of the deadly effects of pesticides is
credited not only with rallying public support against
widespread chemical spraying, but with raising America's
environmental consciousness as well. In *Silent Spring*, Carson, a botanist who died of cancer in 1964, documents in
detail how our reckless use of pesticides has killed not only
targeted insects but all kinds of wildlife and has resulted
in a "silent spring." Carson was among the first to fully
explain the balance of nature and to show how toxics effect
all parts of the food chain, ultimately impacting on man
himself. The connection Carson makes between pesticide
use and the incidence of cancer in humans caused a lot of
controversy and concern, and eventually led to tighter
restrictions on pesticide use.

Foreman, Dave. *ECODEFENSE: A Field Guide to
Monkeywrenching*. 1985. (A Nedd Ludd Book, 1987, second
edition)

Written by Dave Foreman, co-founder of Earth First!,
ECODEFENSE is the practical monkeywrencher's bible.
Replete with photographs and drawings, the book
demonstrates the tried and true techniques of such
ecosabatoge activities as spiking trees, pulling up survey
stakes, downing power lines, and decommissioning heavy
machinery. There are also good chapters on revising
billboard advertiesments (Coca Cola becomes Toxi Cola)
and on basic security precautions. The book is worth reading even if you have no plans to disable a bulldozer. The
short defense of monkeywrenching is as compelling an
argument for the practice as you will find, and, as with
most Earth First!-related projects, the book is highly entertaining. Ed Abbey, who wrote the Forward!, called this "an
essential handbook for those who wish to take part in the
ongoing, last-ditch defense of the little that remains of the
great American wilderness."

Devall, Bill and George Sessions. *Deep Ecology: Living As If
Nature Mattered*.1985. (Peregrine Smith, 1988).

First developed by Norwegian philosopher and environmentalist Arne Naess, the concept of deep ecology refers
to the process of asking "deeper" questions about our
relationship to our surroundings. In *Deep Ecology*, Bill

Devall and George Sessions have done just that. The book deals primarily with the search for a new environmental paradigm, a positive way of looking at and interacting with the world around us. This "Earth wisdom" encourages us to cultivate an "ecological consciousness" by re-examining our Western, egocentric worldview and affirming our interconnectedness with all beings. If this sounds spiritual, it is, and intentionally so. The deep ecology movement sees the spiritual connection as a vital link which has been lost, and which as a consequence, has resulted in our present ecological crisis. *Deep Ecology* is considered by many to be the most important book on the environment to appear within the last decade.

Leopold, Aldo. *A Sand County Almanac.* 1949. (Oxford University Press, 1987).

First published in 1949, this small book remains the classic statement on conservation. In the sketches and essays which make up the Almanac, Leopold, a forest supervisor and biologist, develops his "land ethic". Instead of viewing nature as a commodity to be exploited, Leopold argues that man needs to forge a new relationship with the land based on respect, stewardship, and responsibility. For Leopold, land is a community to which man belongs, and one which needs careful nurturing to endure. Finely crafted and observant, *A Sand Country Almanac* is credited with inspiring generations of environmentalists in their fight to preserve and protect wild places.

McKibben, Bill. *The End of Nature.* 1989. (Random House, 1989).

Touted as the companion to Rachel Carson's *Silent Spring* and Jonathan Schell's *Fate of the Earth*, McKibben's *The End of Nature* is a sobering examination of the greenhouse effect and the environmental crisis in general. It lives up to its advance praise. With great clarity, McKibben discusses the technicalities of global warming and makes it very apparent that our continued burning of fossil fuels will result in drastic changes to life on this planet. The book pulls no punches. Our consuming lifestyles, our addiction to automobiles, and our arrogant, egocentric worldview are to blame for this crisis, which, according to McKibben, may even now be too late to reverse.

Muir, John. *My First Summer in the Sierra.* 1911. (Penguin Books, 1987).

When an aimless wanderer named John Muir first arrived in California in 1868 he took a job tending sheep, herding them from the foothills of the Sierras to the higher elevations of the Tuolumne Meadows. Muir hated the work and the sheep (which he called "a round bundle of something only half alive" and "hooved locusts"), but it gave him the chance to wander through the mountains and gain an education in nature, a experience which would set him on the path of conservation and writing. *My First Summer in the Sierra*, the account of that experience, documents Muir's spiritual conversion to the wild and the beginnings of his love affair with a place he would eventually call home. The book provides good insight into the father of the conservation movement (and the founder of the Sierra Club), and shows just how inspiring nature writing can be.

Thoreau, Henry David. *Walden: Life in the Woods*. 1854. (Penguin, Princeton, American Library, recent editions).

At the age of 27, Thoreau went into the woods near Walden Pond to begin his experiment in "essential living." *Walden* is the record of his experiences, an account of what it was like to live off the land and observe nature firsthand. But it is Thoreau's ruminations on what it is to live a free, independent, and meaningful life that makes *Walden* a lasting source of inspiration. Writing during the rise of the Industrial Revolution, he challenges his readers to break away from a mechanized and conformist society and assume a life of creativity and integrity--not necessarily based on the path Thoreau has chosen, but one which the reader has chosen for himself. *Walden* continues to be essential reading for anyone who wants to lead a live of value, and who seeks to discover the restorative powers of nature.

Worldwatch Institute. *State of the World* (published yearly since 1984). See description above on page 105.

For a comprehensive guide to the major environmental books see Donald Davis' *Ecophilosophy: A Field Guide to the Literature* (R. & E. Miles, 1989). Over 300 of the most influential environmental publications are described in brief, with an emphasis on their contributions to the field and their associations with other works. Davis' Guide is academic in nature--a majority of the works reviewed are highly philosophical--but many are accessible to readers not steeped in the environmental movement. The Guide will help you select pertinent reading, and a perusal of the entries will show you what the major environmental issues are.

ENVIRONMENTAL PUBLICATIONS: Keeping Current

Reading environmental magazines and newspapers is a good way of keeping abreast of what's happening in the environmental movement. Most environmental groups publish an in-house magazine four or six times a year, informing members of their efforts and the state of the environment in general. Some of these, such as the Sierra Club's *Sierra* and the Friends of the Earth's *Not Man Apart*, are especially informative and useful, even for non-members. In recent years, however, a whole slew of independent environmental magazines have hit the stands. The better ones, such as *Buzzworm* and *Garbage*, do a good job of covering the contemporary state of environmental affairs, and tell readers how to take concrete steps to live more responsibly. I have surveyed the major publications and have listed some of the ones that can help you the most.

THE ENVIRONMENTAL NEWSRACK:
The best of the environmental magazines

Buzzworm: The Environmental Journal

Completing its first year of publication, *Buzzworm* has established itself as a premier environmental publication. It's a visual treat, handsomely laid out and filled with striking photographs to accompany the text. But what really sells this magazine is the education it gives you. Feature stories on such topics as endangered species, pollution of the Great Lakes, and the NRA, are highly readable and informative; many end with a list of sources to consult for further information. Regular features are likewise heavy on news you can use--a bulletin board of environmental jobs, a calendar of upcoming events, environmentally-oriented travel opportunities, current news, book reviews, and updates on past stories. Subscriptions are $18/year; six issues. Buzzworm, P.O. Box 6853, Syracuse, NY 13217-7930.

Earth First!: The Radical Environmental Journal

Although it serves as the mouthpiece of the radical environmental group Earth First!, the *Earth First! Journal* reports on news of importance to environmentalists of all ilks. The Journal is particularly strong in its in-depth coverage of the many battles for wilderness preservation taking place across the country, and it provides good philosophical pieces on deep ecology and biodiversity, mainstays of Earth First! thinking. Regular features include discussions of monkeywrenching tactics, international environmental news, updates on EF! projects, book reviews, and irreverent letters to the editor entitled Dear Shit Fer Brains. Subscriptions are $20/year; eight issues. Earth First!, P.O. Box 7, Canton, NY 13617.

Garbage: The Practical Journal for the Environment

One of the newest environmental publications to hit the stands, *Garbage* promises to be a useful, no-nonsense guide for readers who seek to lead environmentally sound lifestyles. Articles in the first two issues looked at the nuts and bolts of composting, cutting home energy bills, recycling, and buying an energy-efficient car. There are also easy-to-understand features on environmental problems, such as global warming, and referrals to sources of information. I find it a little too thin to warrant its subscription rate of $21 for six issues--much of it filled with large graphs and advertisements--but it certainly has the potential to be *the* mainstream environmental magazine. The first two issues completely sold out. Subscriptions are $21/year; six issues. Garbage, P.O. Box 56147, Boulder, CO 80321-1647.

Sierra: The Natural Resource

Sierra is the official publication of the Sierra Club, but its excellent coverage of environmental news makes it a great resource for all environmentalists. The writing is first-rate, and the photography is outstanding and of high quality; the images in the yearly photo contests are always a visual treat. A wide variety of issues are addressed in "In Depth" articles (a recent edition examined laws which govern toxics), and regular features by freelance environmental writers are consistently informative and well researched. *Sierra* is also full of news you can use. The regular "Afield" and "Priorities" features look at the latest trends in environmental news, such as recycling, environmental law, and corporate environmental policies. I can always find useful information in the "Questions & Answers" section on the last page of the magazine. Although I read *Sierra* regularly, I get a little tired of its almost too slick presentation and the proliferation of its advertisements, more than 75 in an issue of some 125 pages! Subscriptions for Sierra Club members are covered by membership dues; nonmember subscriptions are $15/year; six issues. Sierra Club Member Services, P.O. Box 7959, San Francisco, CA 94120-9943.

Utne Reader: The Best of the Alternative Press

Although not specifically an environmental publication, the *Utne Reader* reports regularly on a wide range of environmental topics. The Utne staff is constantly scouring hundreds of alternative publications for the best articles, noting trends and major social concerns. Each issue focuses on a particular subject, and significant portions of the pertinent articles are excerpted. You end up seeing a topic in a single format from many different angles. A recent cover story examined how the environmental crisis could actually improve our lives; other environmental topics covered in past issues include toxics, energy conservation, recycling, the Green movement, ecofeminism, and overpopulation. Subscriptions are $24/year; six issues. Utne Reader, P.O. Box 1974, Marion, OH 43305.

World Watch

This magazine is written by the staff of the Worldwatch Institute, the environmental think tank that publishes the yearly *State of the World*. As a consequence, the articles are on the brainy and analytical side. But don't let that scare you off. The pieces, which resemble short research papers, are very readable and give you the depth not found in most other environmental publications. Some of the topics covered in the past year include grass roots activism, the decommissioning of nuclear power plants, China's family planning policy, and the collapse of the recycled paper market. *World Watch* will give you the substance you need to formulate your environmental beliefs. Subscriptions are $20/year; six issues. Worldwatch Institute, 1776 Massachusetts Avenue, NW, Washington, DC 20036.

ENVIRONMENTAL INFORMATION BY PHONE: Hearing the Day's News

The Legislative Hotline: 202-797-6655

For the price of a phone call, you can listen to a recorded, four-minute update of environmental news and legislation. Offered by the National Wildlife Federation and available 24 hours a day, the Hotline is one of the best ways to get up-to-date information on the status of environmental legislation, as well as names and addresses of groups and elected officials to pressure. A recent message told of James E. Casen's decision to withdraw his name from consideration for the position of Assistant Secretary of

Agriculture, a move hailed by the NWF and other environmental organizations which had labelled Casen "James Watt II". Updates were given on the status of the Oil Spill Liability Bill, the Clean Air Bill, and the World Bank's debate on loans to fund the Sardar Sarovar Dam in India. Listeners were encouraged to attend district meetings with recessing congressional leaders and to write the president of the World Bank, encouraging him to cancel planned loans for the building of the Sardar Sarovar Dam. If you are interested in learning more about any of the topics, you can call the NWF at 202-797-6835, and they will direct you to a specialist in that subject.

ENVIRONMENTAL COMPUTER NETWORK:The Environmental Movement at Your Fingertips

EcoNet

If you have a personal computer and a modem, you can hook up to EcoNet, a computer network for environmentalists. For a monthly charge, users can send electronic mail, gain access to and participate in conferences on environmental issues, and obtain posted information on environmental concerns. The Conference Mode is the most useful avenue for getting information. Several environmental organizations, such as Greenpeace, the Sierra Club, and Friends of the Earth, regularly post notices about environmental legislation, upcoming events, club information, and news events. Conferences are also broken down by subject matter, with scores of topics per subject. There are especially useful and informative subject conferences on recycling, pollution and toxics, energy issues, food and agriculture, climate and atmosphere, and general environmental news. The recycling conference, for instance, lists 105 topics, on everything from styrofoam containers and biodegradable diapers to garbage management in Japan and generating electricity from cow manure. Users are encouraged to respond with their own news or requests for further information. EcoNet also posts alerts and announcements on environmental issues, and maintains a calendar of upcoming events, conferences, and meetings. If you want to keep abreast of what's happening within the environmental community, EcoNet is a valuable, time-saving tool.

Joining EcoNet costs $15 for the initial hook-up and $10 a month, which buys you one hour of free, off-peak connect time (6 pm-7 am weekdays, all weekend hours). Additional off-peak time is $5 an hour; prime connect time is $10.

Contact the Institute for Global Communications, 3228
Sacramento Street, San Francisco, CA 94115; 415-923-0900.

ENVIRONMENTAL TELEVISION PROGRAMS: Nature on the Tube

It has always been pretty easy to find some kind of nature
program on TV. Public television stations regularly air
National Geographic specials, Jacques Cousteau adventures, the Nature series, Nova, and other periodic nature
programs. I grew up watching Marlin Perkins battling
anacondas on Mutual of Omaha's "Wild Kingdom," and
still keep my eyes on the TV guide for the next National
Geographic special. But with the rise in concern about
what we are doing to the environment has come a
proliferation of new, informative, hard-hitting environmental programs. Many have been single segments within
a show, such as Frontline's profile on the toxic pollution
problems of Calvert County, while others are one-time,
independent documentaries. I recommend some of the
many good programs that are out there in the list below.

Discovery Channel programs.

The Discovery Channel, which is available on cable
television, has been airing environmental news for a number of years.

"Earthbeat"

A Ted Turner program, "Earthbeat" dissects environmental issues every Sunday night at 11 o'clock EST on TBS.
Topics have included air pollution, human rights, and
disarmament. The show is trying hard to be not just a news
show, but a forum for personal involvement. Viewers are
encouraged to call a 900 number to voice their opinions on
environmental issues and add their names to "electronic
petitions" that are sent to lawmakers and company execu-
tives. An *Action Guide,* which supplements the information
from each program, is sold individually ($3) or by sub-
scription ($15). Although reviews of the program have
been favorable, the future of "Earthbeat" is in jeopardy. The
show's major sponsor, Thompson Vitamins, has pulled
out due to financial difficulties, forcing TBS to put the
show on hold. For more information contact: Earthbeat,
P.O. Box 7648, Atlanta, GA 30357, 404-874-9696.

ENVIRONMENTAL FILMS/VIDEOS FOR SALE AND RENTAL: The Environment for Film Buffs

A number of the programs listed above, as well as other mainstream and independent environmental films, slideshows, and videotapes, are available for purchase or rental. A good place to start looking is in your local *independent* video store, the more independent and alternative the better. If you don't have any luck, contact Facets (see below), a non-profit arts organization in Chicago, which has a good collection of environmental videos that you can rent (or buy) through the mail. For those of you who are not sure of what's available and want some guidance in selecting good environmental videos, look into *Green Gems* (see below), a guide to the best environmental films and how to get them.

Green Gems

Put together by Environmental Action and Media Network, *Green Gems* is a catalogue of over 100 of the best environmental films, videotapes, and slideshows. Among the topics covered by the films are energy, pollution, agriculture, and the nuclear arms race. The catalogue gives a brief description of the film's content, as well as purchase and rental information. *Green Gems* has been out of print for the last few years--the copy I received was published in 1986--but it is still a good, if out of date, resource on environmental films. I got a copy from Environmental Action for $3.00, but I'm not sure how many they still have in stock. Media Network, which I had trouble reaching, may have more. Contact: Environmental Action, 1525 New Hampshire Ave., NW, Washington, DC 20036, 202-745-4870, or Media Network, 121 Fulton Street, 5th Floor, New York, NY 10038; 212-619-3455.

Facets Multimedia, Inc.

Facets Multimedia, a Chicago-based movie house and video store has one of the largest collections of foreign, classic, and independent American films in the country. They also have a fairly good selection of videotapes on nature and environmental issues. Among its listings are tapes on solar energy, the Audubon Society's guides to birds of North America, Natural Geographic television specials, the adventures of Jacques Cousteau, the Sierra Club Nature series, BBC Wildlife specials, as well as environmental documentaries and how-to guides. You can buy the tapes from Facets or rent them through the mail with a $20 membership. The rental cost is $10 per tape, plus return postage, but you can get a slightly better deal by buying a Critic's membership for $100. As a Critic you get 12 free video-by-mail coupons. A catalogue of Facets' collection is well worth the $4 cost. For more information contact Facets Video, 1517 W. Fullerton Avenue, Chicago, IL 60614; 1-800-331-6197.

The Sierra Club

In partnership with Survival Anglia, the Sierra Club has produced the *Nature Series*, 12 videos on mammals filmed in their natural habitats. Among the animals profiled are tigers, elephants, whales and polar bears. The videos run an hour apiece and are available at video stores. Call 1-800-331-6839 for information on video stores that have them for rent. To purchase the tapes, send $29.95 (plus $2.95 handling for the first tape, $1 for each thereafter) to Kodak, Video Program, P.O. Box 460, Clinton, Tennessee, 37716.

The Sierra Club also rents out a limited selection of films and filmstrips. Their "Filmstrips for Environmental Education" series has six elementary school-level filmstrips, with accompanying soundtracks and fact sheets. The filmstrips, on topics such as John Muir, the interdependence of nature, and Dr. Seuss' "The Lorax," are available for $10 each for a two-week rental. Sierra also rents and sells short, half-hour films on wilderness areas. Most are from the late 1960s to the mid 70s. I remember having seen some of them when I was in grade school. Sale prices are between $150 to $350; rentals are around $15 per day. For more information contact the Sierra Club's Public Affairs department.

part four

the directories

Directory of Environmental Organizations

**CITIZEN'S CLEARINGHOUSE FOR
HAZARDOUS WASTES
P.O. Box 926
Arlington, VA 22216
703-276-7070**

Focus: hazardous wastes
Membership: 17,000 (plus 7,000 member groups)
Dues: $25/year
Publication: quarterly *Everyone's Backyard* and *Action Bulletin*
Status: non-profit; contributions tax-deductible

CCHW is an "environmental crisis center," a clearinghouse for support and information for people concerned about hazardous waste problems in their neighborhoods. Founded by Lois Gibbs, the leader at Love Canal, the group believes that grassroots efforts are the most effective means of bringing about change. Toward that end, CCHW gives people the information and resources they need to wage war against polluters and elected officials. Among the assistance it provides are activist training programs, scientific and technical help, and loads of information on everything from waste disposal sites to the toxic effects of chemicals.

**DEFENDERS OF WILDLIFE
1244 19th St., NW
Washington, DC 20036
202-659-9510**

Focus: wildlife preservation
Membership: 80,000
Dues: $20/year
Publication: bi-monthly *Defenders*

Status: non-profit; contributions tax-deductible

Founded in 1947, Defenders of Wildlife is the primary environmental organization devoted to protecting wildlife and restoring animal and plant life to its natural community. As represented by its logo, the group is most noted for its efforts in support of wolves (it has long been involved in reintroducing the Rocky Mountain wolf into Yellowstone Park); however, Defenders is also active in protecting marine wildlife, the Florida panther, the grizzly bear, and other endangered species. Members can become part of the Defender Activist Network, a support system designed to put pressure on elected officials.

EARTH FIRST!
c/o *Earth First! Journal*
P.O. Box 5871
Tucson, AZ 85703
602-622-1371

Focus: wilderness preservation
Membership: no official membership
Publication: bimonthly *Journal*, subscriptions: $20/year

Unlike the other organizations listed here, Earth First!, exclamation point mandatory, has no official hierarchy or headquarters. It was specifically designed as a movement, not as an organization; anyone can be an Earth First!er. The philosophy of the movement can best be summed up in its adopted motto: "No Compromise In Defense of Mother Earth". In pursuit of this goal, followers commonly practice monkeywrenching, the sabotaging of equipment involved in destroying the environment, as well as other forms of civil disobedience. Belief in deep ecology and biocentrism form the movement's philosophical foundation. The *Earth First! Journal* functions as a forum for the kind of radical environmentalism supported by Earth First!

EARTH ISLAND INSTITUTE
300 Broadway, Suite 28
San Francisco, CA 94133
415-788-3666

Focus: conservation
Membership: 28,000

Dues: $25/year
Publication: quarterly *Earth Island Journal*
Status: non-profit; contributions tax-deductible

This is the most recent project of David Brower, former executive director of the Sierra Club and founder of Friends of the Earth. Established in 1982, Earth Island Institute is a newcomer to the environmental movement, but it has quickly gained respect for its interdisciplinary approach to environmental problems. The Institute's efforts are concentrated primarily on creating and supporting a slew of ongoing projects, everything from the EII annual Fate of the Earth Conference and the Environmental Project on Central America (EPOCA), to the independent efforts of the Green Committees of Correspondence (the group organizing the "Green" political movement in the U.S.). Members receive the *Earth Island Journal*, one of the better in-house environmental publications, which is heavy on international environmental news.

ENVIRONMENTAL DEFENSE FUND
257 Park Avenue South
New York, NY 10010
212-505-2100

Focus: environmental legislation
Membership: 150,000
Dues: $20/year
Publication: bi-monthly *EDF Letter*
Status: non-profit; contributions tax-deductible

One of the more conservative environmental organizations, EDF is known for its staff of paid lawyers who bring lawsuits against polluters and slow-moving regulatory agencies. Litigation plays a big role in EDF's efforts, but the group also supports a growing staff of economists and scientists, who monitor developments within the environmental field and suggest options. One EDF ecologist recently criticized Exxon's use of bacteria in fighting oil spills because of its potential to cause oxygen-depleting algae blooms, and a staff economist spoke to a Polish delegation on using market incentives to control pollution. The group also has an extensive public education program. If you believe the environmental war is best waged through established channels, then EDF is your kind of group.

GREENPEACE U.S.A.
1436 U Street, NW
Washington, DC 20007
202-462-1177

Focus: preservation of wildlife and natural resources
Membership: 850,000
Dues: $20/year
Publication: bi-monthly *Greenpeace*
Status: non-profit; contributions tax-deductible

While not as radical as Earth First! or Sea Shepherds, Greenpeace has developed an image as a tough, front-line group that's not afraid to confront and harass polluters on their own turf. You probably know them as the group whose boat was sunk by French government commandos for invading a nuclear zone, or for the picture of the man parachuting off a smokestack at a coal-fired power plant to protest against acid rain. Direct action with particular attention to media coverage is Greenpeace's forte. The organization has branches around the world, and there are lots of ways to get involved. You can get right in the thick of things by joining direct action campaigns, or you can help with research, drafting of legislation, writing letters, and canvassing, either through Greenpeace U.S.A (the main group) or through Greenpeace Action, its non-profit, more activist-oriented subsidiary.

NATIONAL AUDUBON SOCIETY
950 Third Avenue
New York, NY 10022
212-832-3200

Focus: conservation of wildlife and natural resources
Membership: 550,000
Dues: $20/year
Publication: bi-monthly *Audubon*
Status: non-profit; contributions tax-deductible

Taking its name from the famed ornithologist and artist, John Audubon, the Audubon Society was originally formed as a bird conservation club. And although an interest in the preservation of birds has been an important focus of the group, Audubon supports on-going efforts in the conservation of all wildlife and land resources. It manages a system of 80 sanctuaries, helps establish and protect wildlife refugees and ecological reserves, and engages in the restoration of threatened species. Audubon is particularly strong in public education. In addition to *Audubon* magazine and Audubon Television specials, the group operates education centers, summer ecology camps, and field seminars on natural history and land conservation. Besides supporting these endeavors with your money, you can become an Audubon Activist. Activists receive periodic "action alerts" which inform them of pending legislation and encourage them to contact lawmakers for support. Most of your personal involvement, however, will take place in local chapters, many of which have active conservation committees.

THE NATURE CONSERVANCY
1815 North Lynn Street
Arlington, VA 22209
703-841-5300

Focus: land acquisition; conservation
Membership: 550,000
Dues: $15/year
Publication: bimonthly *The Nature Conservancy Magazine*
Status: non-profit; contributions are tax-deductible

Leaving the political arm-wrestling to other environmental groups, the Nature Conservancy quietly goes about buying up tracts of ecologically important lands. Since its founding in 1951, the group has acquired a total of 3.5 million acres in 50 states, adding on average another thousand acres to that number every day. The Conservancy also supports a staff of scientists, botanists, and zoologists, who identify and catalogue plant and animal life, and work for its preservation. Through local branches, members can volunteer as land stewards, who search for rare plants, check research plots, reintroduce plants, and help with prescribed burns of selected land. Volunteers are also needed to write letters, make phone calls, create computer graphics for newsletters, and for research.

RAINFOREST ACTION NETWORK
301 Broadway, Suite A
San Francisco, CA 94133
415-398-4404

Focus: preservation of rainforests
Membership: 27,000
Dues: $25/year
Publication: quarterly *World Rainforest Report*; monthly *Rainforest Action Network Alert*
Status: non-profit; contributions tax-deductible

RAN believes that the rainforest can be saved by putting pressure on public officials and institutions. After learning that parts of the rainforest were being converted into pasture land for cattle whose meat was being used by American fast-food chains, RAN led a boycott of Burger King--and won. Similar protests have been waged against Scott Paper Company, the Dupont Corporation, and the World Bank, which frequently funds projects that destroy rainforests. Membership in RAN brings you into the *network*, a group of individuals around the world who write letters, lobby, and lead boycotts to protest rainforest destruction. A monthly *Action Alert* keeps you informed of developments and tells you who to write to and what companies to boycott.

SIERRA CLUB
730 Polk Street
San Francisco, CA 94109
415-776-2211

Focus: conservation
Membership: 500,000
Dues: $33/year
Publication: bimonthly *Sierra*
Status: non-profit; contributions are *not* tax-deductible

Founded in 1892 by John Muir, the Sierra Club is one of the largest and most active environmental organizations around. It supports an extensive lobbying force on Capitol Hill which closely monitors environmental legislation, and its position papers have greatly influenced U.S. environmental policy. Unlike many nature groups, the Sierra Club is truly a member's organization. Members are encouraged to actively participate in local chapters, work on task forces, monitor regulatory agencies, publish newsletters, draft position papers, lobby lawmakers, and follow all local environmental issues. Following the example of Muir, the Club also organizes hiking, backpacking, and camping trips. Opportunities for personal involvement are unlimited.

UNITED STATES PUBLIC INTEREST RESEARCH GROUP (U.S. PIRG)
215 Pennsylvania Avenue, SE
Washington, DC 20003
202-546-9707

Focus: consumer and environmental activism
Membership: branches in 17 states
Dues: $25/year
Publication: bimonthly *U.S. PIRG Citizen Agenda*
Status: non-profit; contributions *not* tax-deductible

This is one of the many Ralph Nader-inspired projects, so its focus, not surprisingly, is on research and advocacy. Traditionally, that emphasis has been in consumer rights campaigns; however, with the growing environmental crisis, PIRG has begun addressing environmental concerns--clean air, atmospheric protection, toxic cleanup, and pesticide control. Most of the work is done through state chapters, which define their own agendas, be they bottle bills or clean water acts. These chapters are great places to get involved, especially for students. PIRGS offer summer jobs (campaigning, door-to-door canvassing, researching), some of which can earn you college credit.

THE WILDERNESS SOCIETY
1400 Eye Street, NW
Washington, DC 20005
202-842-3400

Focus: wilderness preservation
Membership: 330,000
Dues: $30
Publication: quarterly *Wilderness*
Status: non-profit; contributions are tax-deductible

The Wilderness Society is in the forefront of organizations looking to create and protect wilderness areas. In doing so, it follows co-founder Aldo Leopold's "land ethic," the conviction that land is a resource, not a commodity. The thrust of the Society's work is primarily political. Its staff continually analyzes the public lands system and works with legislators to protect and preserve the nation's lands. Its current agenda includes protecting the Tongass National Forest, rescuing the wildlife refuges, saving the ancient forests of the Pacific Northwest, and protecting the national parks. Members receive periodic action alerts.

Environmental Service Directory

CO-OP AMERICA
2100 M Street, NW, Suite 310
Washington, DC 20063
202-872-5307

Service: environmentally sound services

Paul Freundlich recognized that people unknowingly buy products from irresponsible companies, and founded Co-op America, an organization that helps consumers put their money where their values are. Its services are as diverse as the ways we spend our money. First, it publishes *The Alternative Catalog,* which profiles hundreds of products--everything from organic pasta and tie-dyed clothing to hand-rolled candles--made by third world cooperatives, minority and worker-owned businesses, and other responsible companies. The group also maintains a brokerage service for IRAs, stocks, and bonds, a health and life insurance company, and a travel agency, all of which are guided by humanistic principles. You must be a member to gain access to Co-op services. Dues are $20/year. Coop-America itself is a non-profit association.

EARTH CARE PAPER, INC.
P.O. Box 3335
Madison, WI 53704
608-256-5522

Service: recycled paper products

Earth Care is one of the many companies looking to "close the loop" in recycling by selling paper products made from recycled paper. Its catalogue is full of attractive recycled alternatives to virgin paper products. In addition to a full range of standard office and printing paper, Earth Care offers wrapping paper, posters, calendars, stationery, lined paper and envelopes, postcards, computer paper, and cellulose food storage bags. A big part of the catalogue is taken up by selections of colorful greeting cards made by the company's freelance artists, who receive royalties from card sales. Earth Care donates 10% of its profits to organizations working to solve environmental and social problems. There is no minimum-sized order. Money back guarantee. Bulk discounts. Order by phone or mail. Catalogue free.

ECO SOLUTIONS
1929 South Fifth St.
Minneapolis, MN 55454
612-338-0250

Service: environmental consulting

Eco Solutions is in the business of helping individuals and their communities to solve the garbage crisis by showing them how to prevent pollution in their day-to-day lives. For Lilias Jones and her crew, information is the key. For the asking, the group will provide you with a slew of articles and booklets on any number of environmental issues: how to conserve water, buy recycled products, preserve wildlife, start a compost pile. It will also give you the names of other organizations to contact. The service is free except for the cost of photocopying and postage. Eco Solutions also offers more extensive assistance in the form of workshops, research, project development, and public education strategies on subjects ranging from waste reduction to sustainable agriculture. Another project in the works is the residential waste survey, which sends a "garbage expert" to inspect your home and help you reduce the amount of trash you create. Eco Solutions is a non-profit organization supported by contributions.

THE ISLAND PRESS
Box 7
Covelo, CA 95428
800-828-1302
FAX: 707-983-6414

Service: environmental publications

The Island Press is a publishing house which specializes in books on environmental topics. It offer nearly 400 titles, on topics ranging from global warming to hazardous waste management and sustainable agriculture. Among its most popular works are Peter Borrelli's *Crossroads: Environmental Priorities for the Future*, Dean Abrahamson's *The Challenge of Global Warming*, and *Environmental Restoration* by John Berger of the Restoring the Earth Project. Island Press also offers environmental books from other publishers. All Island books are printed on recycled, acid-free paper. Money back guarantee. Bulk discounts. Order by phone, mail, or FAX. Catalogue free.

LIVOS PLANT CHEMISTRY
2641 Cerrillos Road
Santa Fe, NM 87501
505-988-9111
FAX: 505-473-0794

Service: non-toxic finishing products

Following a practice it calls "Plant Chemistry," Livos uses only organic, non-toxic ingredients that, when applied as finishes, are harmless to plant and animal life, as well as to soil and water. Among the products offered are oil finishes, wood preservatives, varnishes and shellacs, waxes, paints, primers, and finishes. They also manufacture an organic shoe polish and a variety of children's art supplies, such as crayons, water colors, modelling wax, and finger paints. Samples are available for many of the products. Catalogue free.

REAL GOODS TRADING COMPANY
966 Mazzoni St.
Ukiah, CA 95482
800-762-9214
FAX: 707-468-0301

Service: alternative energy products

Real Goods claims that it offers the "largest and most thorough selection of alternative products in the world." If Real Goods' newsletters and 300-page Alternative Energy Sourcebook are any indication, it would be pretty hard to find anyplace else that gives you more information or a larger selection of energy-saving products. Among its offerings are low-energy appliances (everything from lamps to refrigerators to water heaters), power systems (all kinds of batteries and inverters), and light bulbs, as well as low-flow shower heads and water-conserving toilets (including composting toilets). But Real Goods is really known for its products that harness renewable energy from the sun and wind. Lots of different solar panels and photovoltaic modules are available, as well as wind generators and hydro-electric systems. The Sourcebook, which lists all Real Good products, is great reading, even if you're not planning to buy anything. To find out how to cut your energy costs and to find out what's going on in the alternative energy sector, subscribe to Real Goods. A $20 subscription gets you three newsletters and the annual Sourcebook, plus regular sale mailings. If you don't want to be a member, at least get their Sourcebook for $10. Real Goods promises to beat any price in the USA on any item it sells.

RECYCLED PAPER SOURCES

Conservatree Paper Company
10 Lombard Street
San Francisco, CA 94111
800-522-9200

This is one of the largest companies selling recycled paper. It offers a full line of recycled paper products, including computer paper, letterheads, envelopes, printing papers, newsprint, and copier paper. $100 minimum order.

Earth Care Paper Company
P.O. Box 3335
Madison, WI 53704
608-256-5522

Earth Care offers a full range of standard office and printing paper, plus wrapping paper, posters, calendars, stationery, lined paper and envelopes, postcards, computer paper, and cellulose food storage bags. It has a good selection of colorful greeting cards by company artists. No minimum-sized order.

Ecco Bella
6 Provost Square
Suite 602
Caldwell, NJ 07006
201-226-5799

Ecco Bella sells a full line of unbleached and recycled paper products.

The Paper Project
P.O. Box 12
Arcata, CA 95521
707-822-4338
FAX: 707-826-2136

This company offers recycled paper in a variety of colors, sizes, quality, and types. It sells computer, copier, writing, and office paper; envelopes, stationery, tee shirts, buttons, rubber stamps, and postcards with recycling-oriented messages ("don't throw it away," "once is not enough"). Paper is sold by the carton, ream (500 sheets), or case (5-10 reams according to paper size). Stationery is available in packages of 12 sheets and 8 envelopes.

Recycled Paper Products, Inc.
3636 N. Broadway
Chicago, IL 60613

NOTE: Last year Recycled Paper Products was picketed by a coalition of recyclers who accused the company of not using recycled paper in products advertised as recycled. The company was also accused of using a low percentage of recycled fiber in paper which had been recycled.

RESOURCES CONSERVATION
P.O. Box 71
Greenwich, CT 06836-0071
800-243-2862
FAX: 203-324-9352

Service: water-saving products

Resources Conservation manufactures a number of different water-saving devices. Among its offerings are low-flow shower heads (with and without on/off controls), faucet aerators, and toilet tanks, all through its "Incredible" products line. It also carries the popular Europa low-flow shower heads and other bath fixtures, including adjustable shower arm extenders, spouts, and handles. Free information packet.

RISING SUN ENTERPRISES, INC.
Box 586
Old Snowmass, CO 81654
303-927-8051
FAX: 303-927-3635

Service: energy-efficient lighting, water-saving devices

Founded by former researchers at Rocky Mountain Institute (see below), RSE advises developers and home owners on the latest in resource-efficient technologies. Its catalogue offers an array of compact fluorescent lamps, and light bulbs which use one-fourth the energy of regular bulbs and last ten times longer. RSE also sells a kitchen faucet aerator (with on/off lever) and a bathroom faucet flow control with flow rates of 2.5 g.p.m. and 0.5 g.p.m., respectively. The catalogue costs $3, but it describes each product in detail, and in layman's terms fully explains the technology behind fluorescent lighting.

ROCKY MOUNTAIN INSTITUTE
1739 Snowmass Creek Road
Snowmass, CO 81654
303-927-3851

Service: energy conservation research and publications

Founded in 1982 by renewable entrepreneurs Hunter and Amory Lovins, Rocky Mountain Institute is an environmental think tank dedicated to fostering the use of efficient and sustainable resources. Their research center, a self-sustaining complex on top of a mountain, is a testament to their work. Solar-heating, low-flow shower and faucet heads, water-saving toilets, and superinsulation are just some of the energy-efficient options utilized. RMI staff members focus their research on the areas of agriculture, economic renewal, energy, security, and water, and come up with options and programs for efficiency. Their research is published in RMI papers and books, which are excellent guides for individuals looking to conserve energy. Among the more useful are "Resource-Efficient Housing Guide,"

"Water Efficiency for Your Home," and "Practical Home Energy Savings." A $10 membership gets you RMI's quarterly newsletter, which keeps you up-to-date on the latest energy research and the work of RMI staff members.

SEVENTH GENERATION
Products For A Healthy Planet
10 Farrell Street
S. Burlington, VT 05403
1-800-456-1177

Service: environmentally sound products

Seventh Generation offers a full line of environmentally sound products through its mail order catalogue. Among the offerings are biodegradable plastic bags, cleansers made from natural, non-toxic ingredients, both cloth and biodegradable diapers, organic baby foods, educational toys, recycling containers, water-saving devices, solar appliances, recycled paper, and energy-saving lightbulbs. One percent of gross product sales are donated to non-profit environmental groups. Membership in Seventh Generation entitles you to a 5% discount on all items, a quarterly newsletter, a Seventh Generation tee shirt, and four catalogues during the year. Catalogue $2.00. Money back guarantee. Order by mail, phone, or FAX.

SUN WATT CORPORATION
RFD Box 751
Addison, ME 04606
207-497-2240

Service: solar energy products

A small company based outside of Jonesport, Maine, SunWatt has been producing solar products since 1981. Richard Komp and his associates have focused on photovoltaic modules, marine modules, rechargeable batteries, and battery chargers. The photovoltaic modules and chargers range from the .7 watt type, which can be mounted on a hat and can run a Walkman tapeplayer, to a 10 watt system powerful enough to recharge a 12 volt car battery. The company sells rechargeable batteries, which it claims to be stronger and longer-lasting than regular GE and Radio Shack brands. Richard Komp's guide books to understanding and using solar energy are also available. SunWatt practices what it preaches: the company operates out of a completely self-sufficient facility and uses alternative energy in all of its manufacturing processes. Discounts available. Free catalogue. Order by mail.

TREE SEEDS

Burpee
024497 Burpee Building
Warminster, PA 18974

Burpee carries fruit trees (including dwarfs) and shrubs, as well as 400 different vegetables and 800 varieties of flowers. Catalogue free.

Gurney
Seed & Nursery Co.
Dept. 98-6547A Page Street
Yankton, SD 57079

Gurney offers a good selection of trees and shrubs. Free catalogue.

National Arbor Day Foundation
100 Arbor Avenue
Nebraska City, NE 68410

The Foundation offers a full selection of shade and ornamental trees, flowering shrubs and trees, hedges, fruit trees, nut trees and evergreens. Discount prices for members. Catalogue $2.

Stark Bro's
Nurseries & Orchards Co.
Louisiana, MO 63353-9985

Stark Bro's carries hundreds of varieties of fruit trees (including dwarfs and miniatures). It also has a selection of flowering trees, shade trees, nut trees, hedges, shrubs, and groundcovers. Catalogue free.

The United States Congressional Directory

Congresspersons are listed below by state. Both senators and representatives can be reached either through the legislative offices of their home states (call the state capital for information) or through their Washington offices.

All **senators** can be reached at: United States Senate, Washington, DC 20510; phone for Republicans: 202-224-6391; Democrats: 202-224-8541. All **representatives** can be reached at: United States House of Representatives, Washington, DC 20515; phone for Republicans: 202-225-7350; Democrats: 202-225-7330. Phone numbers to individual offices are listed below, as are FAX numbers, when available. The FAX list is incomplete due to the fact that many congresspersons are reluctant to have these numbers printed.

For information on how to write an effective letter to your Congressperson, see page 92. To get a free copy of this list, contact the Office of Records and Registration at 202-225-1300. The **area code** for all numbers is **202**.

ALABAMA

Senators:

Howell Heflin	OFFICE: 224-4124	FAX:224-3149
Richard C. Shelby	OFFICE: 224-5744	FAX:224-3416

Representatives:

1st	Sonny Callahan	OFFICE: 225-4931	FAX:225-0562
2nd	William L. Dickinson	OFFICE: 225-2901	FAX: unavailable
3rd	Glen Browder	OFFICE: 225-3261	FAX: unavailable

4th	Tom Bevill	OFFICE: 225-4876	FAX: unavailable
5th	Ronnie G. Flippo	OFFICE: 225-4801	FAX: 225-4392
6th	Ben Erdreich	OFFICE: 225-4921	FAX: unavailable
7th	Claude Harris	OFFICE: 225-2665	FAX: 225-0175

ALASKA

Senators:

| | Ted Stevens | OFFICE: 224-3004 | FAX: unavailable |
| | Frank Murkowski | OFFICE: 224-6665 | FAX: unavailable |

Representative:

| | Don Young | OFFICE: 225-5765 | FAX: 225-3208 |

ARIZONA

Senators:

| | Dennis DeConcini | OFFICE: 224-4521 | FAX: 224-8698 |
| | John McCain | OFFICE: 224-2235 | FAX: unavailable |

Representatives:

1st	John J. Rhodes	OFFICE: 225-2635	FAX: 225-0985
2nd	Morris K. Udall	OFFICE: 225-4065	FAX: 225-1176
3rd	Bob Stump	OFFICE: 225-4576	FAX: 225-6328
4th	Jon L. Kyl	OFFICE: 225-3361	FAX: 225-1143
5th	Jim Kolbe	OFFICE: 225-2542	FAX: 225-0378

ARKANSAS

Senators:

| | Dale Bumpers | OFFICE: 224-4843 | FAX: unavailable |
| | David Pryor | OFFICE: 224-2353 | FAX: 224-8261 |

Representatives:

1st	Bill Alexander	OFFICE: 225-4076	FAX: 225-6182
2nd	Tommy F. Robinson	OFFICE: 225-2506	FAX: 225-3646
3rd	John Paul Hammerschmidt	OFFICE: 225-4301	FAX: 225-1141

4th	Beryl Anthony, Jr.	OFFICE: 225-3772	FAX: 225-3646

CALIFORNIA

Senators:

Alan Cranston	OFFICE: 224-3553	FAX: unavailable
Pete Wilson	OFFICE: 224-3841	FAX: unavailable

Representatives:

1st	Douglas H. Bosco	OFFICE: 225-3311	FAX: 225-5577
2nd	Wally Herger	OFFICE: 225-3076	FAX: unavailable
3rd	Robert T. Matsui	OFFICE: 225-7163	FAX: 225-0566
4th	Vic Fazio	OFFICE: 225-5716	FAX: 225-0354
5th	Nancy Pelosi	OFFICE: 225-4965	FAX: 225-8259
6th	Barbara Boxer	OFFICE: 225-5161	FAX: unavailable
7th	George Miller	OFFICE: 225-2095	FAX: 225-5609
8th	Ronald V. Dellums	OFFICE: 225-2661	FAX: 225-9817
9th	Fortney P. Stark	OFFICE: 225-5065	FAX: unavailable
10th	Don Edwards	OFFICE: 225-3072	FAX: 225-9460
11th	Tom Lantos	OFFICE: 225-3531	FAX: 225-3531
12th	Tom. J. Campbell	OFFICE: 225-5411	FAX: 225-5944
13th	Norman Y. Mineta	OFFICE: 225-2631	FAX: unavailable
14th	Norman D. Shumway	OFFICE: 225-2511	FAX: 225-5444
15th	Gary Condit	OFFICE: 225-6131	FAX: 225-0819
16th	Leon E. Panetta	OFFICE: 225-2861	FAX: unavailable
17th	Charles Pashayan, Jr.	OFFICE: 225-3341	FAX: 225-8259
18th	Richard H. Lehman	OFFICE: 225-4540	FAX: unavailable
19th	Robert J. Lagomarsino	OFFICE: 225-3601	FAX: 225-3096
20th	William M. Thomas	OFFICE: 225-2915	FAX: 225-8798
21st	Elton Gallegly	OFFICE: 225-5811	FAX: unavailable
22nd	Carlos J. Moorhead	OFFICE: 225-4176	FAX: 226-1279
23rd	Anthony C. Beilenson	OFFICE: 225-5911	FAX: unavailable
24th	Henry A. Waxman	OFFICE: 225-3976	FAX: 225-4099
25th	Edward R. Roybal	OFFICE: 225-6235	FAX: unavailable
26th	Howard L. Berman	OFFICE: 225-4695	FAX: unavailable
27th	Mel Levine	OFFICE: 225-6451	FAX: 225-6975
28th	Julian C Dixon	OFFICE: 225-7084	FAX: 225-4091

29th	Augustus F. Hawkins	OFFICE: 225-2201	FAX: 225-7854
30th	Matthew G. Martinez	OFFICE: 225-5464	FAX: 225-5467
31st	Mervyn M. Dymally	OFFICE: 225-5425	FAX: 225-6847
32nd	Glenn M. Anderson	OFFICE: 225-6676	FAX: 225-1597
33rd	David Dreier	OFFICE: 225-2305	FAX: unavailable
34th	Esteban Edward Torres	OFFICE: 225-5256	FAX: 225-9711
35th	Jerry Lewis	OFFICE: 225-5861	FAX: 225-6498
36th	George E. Brown, Jr.	OFFICE: 225-6161	FAX: unavailable
37th	Alfred A. McCandless	OFFICE: 225-5330	FAX: 226-1040
38th	Robert K. Dornan	OFFICE: 225-2965	FAX: 225-3694
39th	William E. Dannemeyer	OFFICE: 225-4111	FAX: unavailable
40th	C. Christopher Cox	OFFICE: 225-5611	FAX: 255-9177
41st	Bill Lowery	OFFICE: 225-3201	FAX: 225-7383
42nd	Dana Rohrabacher	OFFICE: 225-2415	FAX: 225-0145
43rd	Ron Packard	OFFICE: 225-3906	FAX: 225-0134
44th	Jim Bates	OFFICE: 225-5452	FAX: 225-2558
45th	Duncan Hunter	OFFICE: 225-5672	FAX: 225-0235

COLORADO

Senators:

William L. Armstrong	OFFICE: 224-5941	FAX: unavailable
Timothy E. Wirth	OFFICE: 224-5852	FAX: unavailable

Representatives:

1st	Patricia Schroeder	OFFICE: 225-4431	FAX: 225-5842
2nd	David E. Skaggs	OFFICE: 225-2161	FAX: unavailable
3rd	Ben N. Campbell	OFFICE: 225-4761	FAX: 225-0228
4th	Hank Brown	OFFICE: 225-4676	FAX: 225-8630
5th	Joel Hefley	OFFICE: 225-4422	FAX: 225-1942
6th	Dan Schaefer	OFFICE: 225-7882	FAX: 225-7885

CONNECTICUT

Senators:

Joseph I. Lieberman	OFFICE: 224-4041	FAX: 224-9750
Christopher J. Dodd	OFFICE: 224-2823	FAX: unavailable

Representatives:

1st	Barbara B. Kennelly	OFFICE: 225-2265	FAX: 225-1031
2nd	Samuel Gejdenson	OFFICE: 225-2076	FAX: unavailable
3rd	Bruce A. Morrison	OFFICE: 225-3661	FAX: unavailable
4th	Christopher Shays	OFFICE: 225-5541	FAX: 225-9629
5th	John G. Rowland	OFFICE: 225-3822	FAX: 225-5085
6th	Nancy L. Johnson	OFFICE: 225-4476	FAX: 225-4488

DELAWARE

Senators:

William V. Roth, Jr.	OFFICE: 224-2441	FAX: unavailable
Joseph R. Biden, Jr.	OFFICE: 224-5042	FAX: unavailable

Representative:

Thomas R. Carper	OFFICE: 225-4165	FAX: 225-1912

FLORIDA

Senators:

Connie Mack	OFFICE: 224-5274	FAX: 224-9365
Bob Graham	OFFICE: 224-3041	FAX: unavailable

Representatives:

1st	Earl Hutto	OFFICE: 225-4136	FAX: 225-5785
2nd	Bill Grant	OFFICE: 225-5235	FAX: 225-1586
3rd	Charles E. Bennett	OFFICE: 225-2501	FAX: 225-9635
4th	Craig T. James	OFFICE: 225-4035	FAX: unavailable
5th	Bill McCollum	OFFICE: 225-2176	FAX: unavailable
6th	Clifford Stearns	OFFICE: 225-5744	FAX: unavailable
7th	Sam M. Gibbons	OFFICE: 225-3376	FAX: unavailable
8th	C. W. (Bill) Young	OFFICE: 225-5961	FAX: 225-9764
9th	Michael Bilirakis	OFFICE: 225-5755	FAX: 225-4085
10th	Andy Ireland	OFFICE: 225-5015	FAX: 225-6944
11th	Bill Nelson	OFFICE: 225-3671	FAX: 225-9039
12th	Tom Lewis	OFFICE: 225-5792	FAX: 225-1860
13th	Porter J. Goss	OFFICE: 225-2536	FAX: 225-6820

14th	Harry Johnston, III	OFFICE: 225-3001	FAX: 225-8791
15th	E. Clay Shaw, Jr.	OFFICE: 225-3026	FAX: 225-8398
16th	Lawrence J. Smith	OFFICE: 225-7931	FAX: 225-9816
17th	William Lehman	OFFICE: 225-4211	FAX: 225-6208
18th	Ileana Ros-Lehtinen	OFFICE:225-3931	FAX :unavailable
19th	Dante B. Fascell	OFFICE: 225-4506	FAX: 225-0724

GEORGIA

Senators:

| | Sam Nunn | OFFICE: 224-3521 | FAX: 224-0072 |
| | Wyche Fowler, Jr. | OFFICE: 224-3643 | FAX: 224-8227 |

Representatives:

1st	Robert Thomas	OFFICE: 225-5831	FAX: 225-6922
2nd	Charles Hatcher	OFFICE: 225-3631	FAX: 225-1117
3rd	Richard Ray	OFFICE: 225-5901	FAX: 225-1598
4th	Ben Jones	OFFICE: 225-4272	FAX: 225-8675
5th	John Lewis	OFFICE: 225-3801	FAX: 225-0351
6th	Newt Gingrich	OFFICE: 225-4501	FAX: 225-4656
7th	George (Buddy) Darden	OFFICE: 225-2931	FAX: unavailable
8th	J. Roy Rowland	OFFICE: 225-6531	FAX: unavailable
9th	Ed Jenkins	OFFICE:225-5211	FAX: unavailable
10th	Doug Barnard, Jr.	OFFICE: 225-4101	FAX: 225-1873

HAWAII

Senators:

| | Daniel K. Inouye | OFFICE: 224-3934 | FAX: 224-6747 |
| | Spark M. Matsunaga | OFFICE: 224-6361 | FAX: unavailable |

Representatives:

| 1st | Patricia Saiki | OFFICE: 225-2726 | FAX: 225-4580 |
| 2nd | Daniel K. Akaka | OFFICE: 225-4906 | FAX: 225-4987 |

IDAHO

Senators:

James A. McClure	OFFICE:224-2752	FAX: unavailable
Steve Symms	OFFICE: 224-6142	FAX: 224-5893

Representatives:

1st	Larry E. Craig	OFFICE: 225-6611	FAX: 226-1213
2nd	Richard H. Stallings	OFFICE: 225-5531	FAX: unavailable

ILLINOIS

Senators:

Alan Dixon	OFFICE: 224-2854	FAX: 224-5581
Paul Simon	OFFICE: 224-2152	FAX: unavailable

Representatives:

1st	Charles A. Hayes	OFFICE: 225-4372	FAX: unavailable
2nd	Gus Savage	OFFICE: 225-0773	FAX: 226-8608
3rd	Marty Russo	OFFICE: 225-5736	FAX: 225-0295
4th	George Sangmeister	OFFICE: 225-3635	FAX: 225-4447
5th	William O. Lipinksi	OFFICE: 225-5701	FAX: 225-1012
6th	Henry J. Hyde	OFFICE: 225-4561	FAX: 226-1240
7th	Cardiss Collins	OFFICE: 225-5006	FAX: 225-8396
8th	Dan Rostenkowski	OFFICE: 225-4061	FAX: 225-6064
9th	Sidney R. Yates	OFFICE: 225-2111	FAX: 225-3493
10th	John Edward Porter	OFFICE: 225-4835	FAX: 225-0157
11th	Frank Annunzio	OFFICE: 225-6661	FAX: unavailable
12th	Philip M. Crane	OFFICE: 225-3711	FAX: unavailable
13th	Harris W. Fawell	OFFICE: 225-3515	FAX: 225-9240
14th	J. Dennis Hastert	OFFICE: 225-2976	FAX: 225-0697
15th	Edward R. Madigan	OFFICE: 225-2371	FAX: unavailable
16th	Lynn Martin	OFFICE: 225-5676	FAX: unavailable
17th	Lane Evans	OFFICE: 225-5905	FAX: 225-5396
18th	Robert H. Michel	OFFICE: 225-6201	FAX: 225-9461
19th	Terry L. Bruce	OFFICE: 225-5001	FAX: 225-9810
20th	Richard J. Durbin	OFFICE: 225-5271	FAX: unavailable
21st	Jerry F. Costello	OFFICE: 225-5661	FAX: 225-0285

22nd Glen Poshard   OFFICE: 225-5201   FAX: 225-1541

INDIANA

Senators:

Richard G. Lugar   OFFICE: 224-4814   FAX: unavailable

Representatives:

1st	Peter J. Visclosky	OFFICE: 225-2461	FAX: unavailable
2nd	Philip R. Sharp	OFFICE: 225-3021	FAX: unavailable
3rd	John Hiler	OFFICE: 225-3915	FAX: unavailable
4th	Jill Long	OFFICE: 225-4436	FAX: unavailable
5th	Jim Jontz	OFFICE: 225-5037	FAX: unavailable
6th	Dan Burton	OFFICE: 225-2276	FAX: unavailable
7th	John T. Myers	OFFICE: 225-5805	FAX: unavailable
8th	Frank McCloskey	OFFICE: 225-4636	FAX: unavailable
9th	Lee H. Hamilton	OFFICE: 225-5315	FAX: unavailable
10th	Andrew Jacobs, Jr.	OFFICE: 225-4011	FAX: unavailable

IOWA

Senators:

Charles E. Grassley   OFFICE: 224-3744   FAX: unavailable
Tom Harkin   OFFICE: 224-3254   FAX: unavailable

Representatives:

1st	Jim Leach	OFFICE: 225-6576	FAX: unavailable
2nd	Thomas J. Tauke	OFFICE: 225-2911	FAX: unavailable
3rd	David R. Nagle	OFFICE: 225-3301	FAX: unavailable
4th	Neal Smith	OFFICE: 225-4426	FAX: unavailable
5th	Jim Lightfoot	OFFICE: 225-3806	FAX: unavailable
6th	Fred Grandy	OFFICE: 225-5476	FAX: unavailable

KANSAS

Senators:

Robert Dole	OFFICE: 224-6521	FAX: 224-8952
Nancy Landon Kassebaum	OFFICE: 224-4774	FAX: 224-3514

Representatives:

1st	Pat Roberts	OFFICE: 225-2715	FAX: 225-5375
2nd	Jim Slattery	OFFICE: 225-6601	FAX: unavailable
3rd	Jan Meyers	OFFICE: 225-2865	FAX: 225-0554
4th	Dan Glickman	OFFICE: 225-6216	FAX: unavailable
5th	Robert Whittaker	OFFICE: 225-3911	FAX: unavailable

KENTUCKY

Senators:

Wendell H. Ford	OFFICE: 224-4343	FAX: unavailable
Mitch McConnell	OFFICE: 224-2541	FAX: 224-2499

Representatives:

1st	Carroll Hubbard, Jr.	OFFICE: 225-3115	FAX: 225-1622
2nd	William H. Natcher	OFFICE: 225-3501	FAX: unavailable
3rd	Romano L. Mazzoli	OFFICE: 225-5401	FAX: unavailable
4th	Jim Bunning	OFFICE: 225-3465	FAX: 225-0003
5th	Harold Rogers	OFFICE: 225-4601	FAX: 225-0940
6th	Larry J. Hopkins	OFFICE: 225-4706	FAX: 225-1413
7th	Carl C. Perkins	OFFICE: 225-4935	FAX: unavailable

LOUISIANA

Senators:

Bennett J. Johnston	OFFICE: 224-5824	FAX: 224-2501
John B. Breaux	OFFICE: 224-4623	FAX: 224-9753

Representatives:

1st	Bob Livingston	OFFICE: 225-3015	FAX: 225-0739
2nd	Lindy Boggs	OFFICE: 226-6636	FAX: 226-1239
3rd	Billy Tauzin	OFFICE: 225-4031	FAX: unavaliable

4th	Jim McCrery	OFFICE: 225-2777	FAX: 225-8039
5th	Jerry Huckaby	OFFICE: 225-2376	FAX: 225-2387
6th	Richard H. Baker	OFFICE: 225-3901	FAX: 225-7313
7th	James A. Hayes	OFFICE: 225-2031	FAX: 225-7571
8th	Clyde C. Holloway	OFFICE: 225-4926	FAX: 225-6252

MAINE

Senators:

| | William S. Cohen | OFFICE: 224-2523 | FAX: unavailable |
| | George J. Mitchell | OFFICE: 224-5344 | FAX: unavailable |

Representatives:

| 1st | Joseph E. Brennan | OFFICE: 225-6116 | FAX: 225-9065 |
| 2nd | Olympia J. Snowe | OFFICE: 225-6306 | FAX: 225-8880 |

MARYLAND

Senators:

| | Paul S. Sarbanes | OFFICE: 224-4524 | FAX: 224-1651 |
| | Barbara A. Mikulski | OFFICE: 224-4654 | FAX: 224-8858 |

Representatives:

1st	Roy Dyson	OFFICE: 225-5311	FAX: 225-0254
2nd	Helen Delich Bentley	OFFICE: 225-3061	FAX: 225-4251
3rd	Benjamin L. Cardin	OFFICE: 225-4016	FAX: 225-9219
4th	C. Thomas McMillen	OFFICE: 225-8090	FAX: 225-8099
5th	Steny H. Hoyer	OFFICE: 225-4131	FAX: 225-4300
6th	Beverly B. Byron	OFFICE: 225-2721	FAX: 225-6159
7th	Kweisi Mfume	OFFICE: 225-4741	FAX: unavailable
8th	Constance A. Morella	OFFICE: 225-5341	FAX: 225-1389

MASSACHUSETTS

Senators:

| | Edward M. Kennedy | OFFICE: 224-4543 | FAX: 224-2417 |
| | John F. Kerry | OFFICE: 224-2742 | FAX: 224-8525 |

Representatives:

1st	Silvio O. Conte	OFFICE: 225-5335	FAX: 225-8112
2nd	Richard E. Neal	OFFICE: 225-5601	FAX: 225-8112
3rd	Joseph D. Early	OFFICE: 225-6101	FAX: 225-3181
4th	Barney Frank	OFFICE: 225-5931	FAX: unavailavle
5th	Chester G. Atkins	OFFICE: 225-3411	FAX: unavailable
6th	Nicholas Mavroules	OFFICE: 225-8020	FAX: 225-8023
7th	Edward J. Markey	OFFICE: 225-2836	FAX: unavailable
8th	Joseph P. Kennedy II	OFFICE: 225-5111	FAX: 225-9322
9th	John Joseph	OFFICE: 225-8273	FAX: 225-7804
10th	Gerry E. Studds	OFFICE: 225-3111	FAX: unavailable
11th	Brian J. Donnelly	OFFICE: 225-3215	FAX: unavailable

MICHIGAN

Senators:

Donald W. Riegle, Jr.	OFFICE: 224-4822	FAX: 224-8834
Carl Levin	OFFICE: 224-6221	FAX: unavailable

Representatives:

1st	John Conyers, Jr.	OFFICE: 225-5126	FAX: 225-0072
2nd	Carl D. Pursell	OFFICE: 225-4401	FAX: unavailable
3rd	Howard Wolpe	OFFICE: 225-5011	FAX: 225-8602
4th	Frederick S. Upton	OFFICE: 225-3761	FAX: 225-4986
5th	Paul B. Henry	OFFICE: 225-3831	FAX: unavailable
6th	Bob Carr	OFFICE: 225-4872	FAX: 225-1260
7th	Dale E. Kildee	OFFICE: 225-3611	FAX: 225-3692
8th	Bob Traxler	OFFICE: 225-2806	FAX: 225-3046
9th	Guy Vander Jagt	OFFICE: 225-3511	FAX: unavailable
10th	Bill Schuette	OFFICE: 225-3561	FAX: 225-6971
11th	Robert W. Davis	OFFICE: 225-4735	FAX: 225-3588
12th	David E. Bonior	OFFICE: 225-2106	FAX: 226-1169
13th	George W. Crockett Jr.	OFFICE: 225-2261	FAX: unavailable
14th	Dennis M. Hertel	OFFICE: 225-6276	FAX: unavailable
15th	William D. Ford	OFFICE: 225-6261	FAX: unavailable
16th	John D. Dingell	OFFICE: 225-4071	FAX: 225-7426

| 17th | Sander M. Levin | OFFICE: 225-4961 | FAX: unavailable |
| 18th | William S. Broomfield | OFFICE: 225-6135 | FAX: 225-1807 |

MINNESOTA

Senators:

| | David Durenberger | OFFICE: 224-3244 | FAX: unavailable |
| | Rudy Boschwitz | OFFICE: 224-5641 | FAX: 224-8438 |

Representatives:

1st	Timothy J. Penny	OFFICE: 225-2472	FAX: 225-0051
2nd	Vin Weber	OFFICE: 225-2331	FAX: 225-0987
3rd	Bill Frenzel	OFFICE: 225-2871	FAX: 225-6351
4th	Bruce F. Vento	OFFICE: 225-6631	FAX: 225-1968
5th	Martin O. Sabo	OFFICE: 225-4755	FAX: unavailable
6th	Gerry Sikorski	OFFICE: 225-2271	FAX: 225-4347
7th	Arlan Stangeland	OFFICE: 225-2165	FAX: 225-1593
8th	James L. Oberstar	OFFICE: 225-6211	FAX: 225-0699

MISSISSIPPI

Senators:

| | Trent Lott | OFFICE: 224-6253 | FAX: 224-2262 |
| | Thad Cochran | OFFICE: 224-5054 | FAX: unavailable |

Representatives:

1st	Jamie L. Whitten	OFFICE: 225-4306	FAX: 225-4328
2nd	Mike Espy	OFFICE: 225-5876	FAX: 225-5898
3rd	G.V. Sonny Montgomery	OFFICE: 225-5031	FAX: unavailable
4th	Mike Parker	OFFICE: 225-5865	FAX: 225-5886
5th	Larkin Smith	OFFICE: 225-5772	FAX: 225-7074

MISSOURI

Senators:

| | John C. Danforth | OFFICE: 224-6154 | FAX: 224-7615 |
| | Christopher (Kit) Bond | OFFICE: 224-5721 | FAX: 224-8149 |

Representatives:

1st	William L. Clay	OFFICE: 225-2406	FAX: 225-1783
2nd	Jack Buechner	OFFICE: 225-2561	FAX: 225-1378
3rd	Richard A. Gephardt	OFFICE: 225-2671	FAX: 225-7452
4th	Ike Skelton	OFFICE: 225-2876	FAX: 225-2695
5th	Alan Wheat	OFFICE: 225-4535	FAX: unavailable
6th	E. Thomas Coleman	OFFICE: 225-7041	FAX: 225-4799
7th	Mel Hancock	OFFICE: 225-6536	FAX: 225-7700
8th	Bill Emerson	OFFICE: 225-4404	FAX: 225-9621
9th	Harold L. Volkmer	OFFICE: 225-2956	FAX: 225-7834

MONTANA

Senators:

| | Conrad Burns | OFFICE: 224-2644 | FAX: 224-8594 |
| | Max Baucus | OFFICE: 224-2651 | FAX: unavailable |

Representatives:

| 1st | Pat Williams | OFFICE: 225-3211 | FAX: 225-1257 |
| 2nd | Ron Marlenee | OFFICE: 225-1555 | FAX: 225-1558 |

NEBRASKA

Senators:

| | J. James Exon | OFFICE: 224-4224 | FAX: 224-5213 |
| | Robert Kerrey | OFFICE: 224-6551 | FAX: 224-7645 |

Representatives:

1st	Doug Bereuter	OFFICE: 225-4806	FAX: 226-1148
2nd	Peter Hoagland	OFFICE: 225-4155	FAX: 225-4684
3rd	Virginia Smith	OFFICE: 225-6435	FAX: 225-0207

NEVADA

Senators:

Richard H. Bryan	OFFICE: 224-6244	FAX: 224-1867
Harry Reid	OFFICE: 224-3542	FAX: unavailable

Representatives:

1st	James H. Bilbray	OFFICE: 225-5965	FAX: 225-8808
2nd	Barbara F. Vucanovich	OFFICE: 225-6155	FAX: 225-2319

NEW HAMPSHIRE

Senators:

Gordon J. Humphrey	OFFICE: 224-2841	FAX: 224-1353
Warren B. Rudman	OFFICE: 224-3324	FAX: unavailable

Representatives:

1st	Robert C. Smith	OFFICE: 225-5456	FAX: unavailable
2nd	Charles Douglas III	OFFICE: 225-5206	FAX: 225-0046

NEW JERSEY

Senators:

Bill Bradley	OFFICE: 224-3224	FAX: 224-8567
Frank R. Lautenberg	OFFICE: 224-4744	FAX: 224-9707

Representatives:

1st	James J. Florio	OFFICE: 225-6501	FAX: unavailable
2nd	William J. Hughes	OFFICE: 225-6572	FAX: 226-1108
3rd	Frank Pallone, Jr.	OFFICE: 225-4671	FAX: 225-9665
4th	Christopher H. Smith	OFFICE: 225-3765	FAX: 225-7768
5th	Marge Roukema	OFFICE: 225-4465	FAX: 225-9048
6th	Bernard J. Dwyer	OFFICE: 225-6301	FAX: 225-1553
7th	Matthew J. Rinaldo	OFFICE: 225-5361	FAX: 225-5679
8th	Robert A. Roe	OFFICE: 225-5751	FAX: 225-3071
9th	Robert G. Torricelli	OFFICE: 225-5061	FAX: 225-0843
10th	Donald M. Payne	OFFICE: 225-3436	FAX: unavailable
11th	Dean A. Gallo	OFFICE: 225-5034	FAX: 225-0658

12th	James Courter	OFFICE: 225-5801	FAX: 225-9181
13th	H. James Saxton	OFFICE: 225-4765	FAX: 225-0778
14th	Frank J. Guarini	OFFICE: 225-2765	FAX: 225-7023

NEW MEXICO

Senators:

| | Pete V. Domenici | OFFICE: 224-6621 | FAX: 224-7371 |
| | Jeff Bingaman | OFFICE: 224-5521 | FAX: unavailable |

Representatives:

1st	Steven H. Schiff	OFFICE: 225-6316	FAX: 225-4975
2nd	Joe Skeen	OFFICE: 225-2365	FAX: 225-9599
3rd	Bill Richardson	OFFICE: 225-6190	FAX: unavailable

NEW YORK

Senators:

| | Daniel P. Moynihan | OFFICE: 224-4451 | FAX: unavailable |
| | Alfonse M. D'Amato | OFFICE: 224-6542 | FAX: 224-5871 |

Representatives:

1st	George J. Hochbrueckner	OFFICE: 225-3826	FAX: 225-0776
2nd	Thomas J. Downey	OFFICE: 225-3335	FAX: 226-1275
3rd	Robert J. Mrazek	OFFICE: 225-5956	FAX: 225-7215
4th	Norman F. Lent	OFFICE: 225-7896	FAX: 225-0357
5th	Raymond J. McGrath	OFFICE: 225-5516	FAX: 225-3625
6th	Floyd H. Flake	OFFICE: 225-3461	FAX: 226-4169
7th	Gary L. Ackerman	OFFICE: 225-2601	FAX: 225-1589
8th	James H. Scheuer	OFFICE: 225-5471	FAX: 225-9695
9th	Thomas J. Manton	OFFICE: 225-3965	FAX: 225-1452
10th	Charles E. Schumer	OFFICE: 225-6616	FAX: 225-4183
11th	Edolphus Towns	OFFICE: 225-5936	FAX: 225-1018
12th	Major R. Owens	OFFICE: 225-6231	FAX: unavailable
13th	Stephen J. Solarz	OFFICE: 225-2361	FAX: 225-9496
14th	Guy V. Molinari	OFFICE: 225-3371	FAX: 226-1272
15th	Bill Green	OFFICE: 225-2436	FAX: 225-0840

16th	Charles B. Rangel	OFFICE: 225-4365	FAX: 225-0816
17th	Ted Weiss	OFFICE: 225-5635	FAX: 225-6923
18th	Robert Garcia	OFFICE: 225-4361	FAX: unavailable
19th	Eliot L. Engel	OFFICE: 225-2464	FAX: unavailable
20th	Nita M. Lowey	OFFICE: 225-6506	FAX: 225-0546
21st	Hamilton Fish, Jr.	OFFICE: 225-5441	FAX: 225-0962
22nd	Benjamin A. Gilman	OFFICE:225-3776	FAX: 225-9636
23rd	Michael R. McNulty	OFFICE: 225-5076	FAX: unavailable
24th	Gerald B. Solomon	OFFICE: 225-5614	FAX: 225-1668
25th	Sherwood L. Boehlert	OFFICE: 225-3665	FAX: 225-1891
26th	David O'B. Martin	OFFICE: 225-4611	FAX: unavailable
27th	James T. Walsh	OFFICE: 225-3701	FAX: 225-4042
28th	Matthew F. McHugh	OFFICE: 225-6335	FAX: 225-1799
29th	Frank Horton	OFFICE: 225-4916	FAX: 225-5909
30th	Louise Slaughter	OFFICE: 225-3615	FAX: 225-7822
31st	William Paxon	OFFICE: 225-5265	FAX: 225-5910
32nd	John J. LaFalce;	OFFICE: 225-3231	FAX: 225-8693
33rd	Henry J. Nowak	OFFICE: 225-3306	FAX: 225-3523
34th	Amory Houghton, Jr.	OFFICE: 225-3161	FAX: 225-5574

NORTH CAROLINA

Senators:

	Jesse Helms	OFFICE: 224-6342	FAX: 224-1376
	Terry Sanford	OFFICE: 224-3154	FAX: 224-7406

Representatives:

1st	Walter B. Jones	OFFICE: 225-3101	FAX: unavailable
2nd	Tim Valentine, Jr.	OFFICE: 225-4531	FAX: 225-1539
3rd	H. Martin Lancaster	OFFICE: 225-3415	FAX: 225-0666
4th	David E. Price	OFFICE: 225-1784	FAX: 225-6314
5th	Stephen L. Neal	OFFICE: 225-2071	FAX: 225-4060
6th	Howard Coble	OFFICE: 225-3065	FAX: 225-8611
7th	Charles Rose	OFFICE: 225-2731	FAX: 225-2470
8th	W. G. Bill Hefner	OFFICE: 225-3715	FAX: 225-4036
9th	Alex McMillan	OFFICE: 225-1976	FAX: 225-8995
10th	Cass Ballenger	OFFICE: 225-2576	FAX: 225-0316

11th	James McClure Clarke	OFFICE: 225-6401	FAX: 225-0519

NORTH DAKOTA

Senators:

Quentin N. Burdick	OFFICE: 224-2611	FAX: unavailable
Kent Conrad	OFFICE: 224-2043	FAX: unavailable

Representative:

Byron L. Dorgan	OFFICE: 225-2611	FAX: unavailable

OHIO

Senators:

John Glenn	OFFICE: 224-3353	FAX: unavailable
Howard M. Metzenbaum	OFFICE: 224-2315	FAX: 224-8906

Representatives:

1st	Thomas A. Luken	OFFICE: 225-2216	FAX: 225-2293
2nd	Willis D. Gradison, Jr.	OFFICE: 225-3164	FAX: unavailable
3rd	Tony P. Hall	OFFICE: 225-6465	FAX: 225-6766
4th	Michael G. Oxley	OFFICE: 225-2676	FAX: unavailable
5th	Paul E. Gillmor	OFFICE: 225-6405	FAX: unavailable
6th	Bob McEwen	OFFICE: 225-5705	FAX: 225-0224
7th	Michael DeWine	OFFICE: 225-4324	FAX: unavailable
8th	Donald E. (Buz) Lukens	OFFICE: 225-6205	FAX: 225-0704
9th	Marcy Kaptur	OFFICE: 225-4146	FAX: 225-7711
10th	Clarence E. Miller	OFFICE: 225-5131	FAX: 225-5132
11th	Dennis E. Eckart	OFFICE: 225-6331	FAX: 225-1514
12th	John R. Kasich	OFFICE: 225-5355	FAX: unavailable
13th	Donald J. Pease	OFFICE: 225-3401	FAX: 225-0066
14th	Thomas C. Sawyer	OFFICE: 225-5231	FAX: 225-5278
15th	Chalmers P. Wylie	OFFICE: 225-2015	FAX: 225-7548
16th	Ralph Regula	OFFICE: 225-3876	FAX: 225-3095
17th	James A. Traficant, Jr.	OFFICE: 225-5261	FAX: 225-3719
18th	Douglas Applegate	OFFICE: 225-6265	FAX: 225-3087
19th	Edward F. Feighan	OFFICE: 225-5731	FAX: 226-1230

| **20th** | Mary Rose Oakar | OFFICE: 225-5871 | FAX: 225-0663 |
| **21st** | Louis Stokes | OFFICE: 225-7032 | FAX: 225-1339 |

OKLAHOMA

Senators:

| | David L. Boren | OFFICE: 224-4721 | FAX: 224-0154 |
| | Don Nickles | OFFICE: 224-5754 | FAX: unavailable |

Representatives:

1st	James M. Inhofe	OFFICE: 225-2211	FAX: 225-9187
2nd	Mike Synar	OFFICE: 225-2701	FAX: 225-2796
3rd	Wes Watkins	OFFICE: 225-4565	FAX: 225-9029
4th	Dave McCurdy	OFFICE: 225-6165	FAX: unavailable
5th	Mickey Edwards	OFFICE: 225-2132	FAX: unavailable
6th	Glenn English	OFFICE: 225-5565	FAX: 225-8698

OREGON

Senators:

| | Mark O. Hatfield | OFFICE: 224-3753 | FAX: unavailable |
| | Bob Packwood | OFFICE: 224-5244 | FAX: 224-5244 |

Representatives:

1st	Les AuCoin	OFFICE: 225-0855	FAX: 225-2707
2nd	Robert F. (Bob) Smith	OFFICE: 225-6730	FAX: 225-3129
3rd	Ron Wyden	OFFICE: 225-4811	FAX: unavailable
4th	Peter A. DeFazio	OFFICE: 225-6416	FAX: 225-0694
5th	Denny Smith	OFFICE: 225-5711	FAX: unavailable

PENNSYLVANIA

Senators:

| | John Heinz | OFFICE: 224-6324 | FAX: 224-7763 |
| | Arlen Specter | OFFICE: 224-4254 | FAX: unavailable |

Representatives:

1st	Thomas M. Foglietta	OFFICE: 225-4731	FAX: unavailable
2nd	William H. Gray, III	OFFICE: 225-4001	FAX: 225-2995
3rd	Robert A. Borski, Jr.	OFFICE: 225-8251	FAX: 225-4628
4th	Joseph Kolter	OFFICE: 225-2565	FAX: 225-0526
5th	Richard T. Schulze	OFFICE: 225-5761	FAX: unavailable
6th	Gus Yatron	OFFICE: 225-5546	FAX: 225-5548
7th	Curt Weldon	OFFICE: 225-2011	FAX: 225-8137
8th	Peter H. Kostmayer	OFFICE: 225-4276	FAX: 225-5060
9th	Bud Shuster	OFFICE: 225-2431	FAX: unavailable
10th	Joseph M. McDade	OFFICE: 225-3731	FAX: 225-9594
11th	Paul E. Kanjorski	OFFICE: 225- 6511	FAX: unavailable
12th	John P. Murtha	OFFICE: 225-2065	FAX: 225-5709
13th	Lawrence Coughlin	OFFICE: 225-6111	FAX: unavailable
14th	William J. Coyne	OFFICE: 225-2301	FAX: 225-1844
15th	Don Ritter	OFFICE: 225-6411	FAX: unavailable
16th	Robert S. Walker	OFFICE: 225-2411	FAX: 225-2484
17th	George W. Gekas	OFFICE: 225-4315	FAX: 225-8440
18th	Doug Walgren	OFFICE: 225-2135	FAX: 225-7747
19th	William F. Goodling	OFFICE: 225-5836	FAX: 225-1000
20th	Joseph M. Gaydos	OFFICE: 225-4631	FAX: unavailable
21st	Thomas J. Ridge	OFFICE: 225-5406	FAX: 225-1081
22nd	Austin J. Murphy	OFFICE: 225-4665	FAX: 225-4772
23rd	William F. Clinger, Jr	OFFICE: 225-5121	FAX: 225-4681

RHODE ISLAND

Senators:

Claiborne Pell	OFFICE: 224-4642	FAX: 224-4680
John H. Chafee	OFFICE: 224-2921	FAX: 224-6166

Representatives:

1st	Ronald K. Machtley	OFFICE: 225-4911	FAX: unavailable
2nd	Claudine Schneider	OFFICE: 225-2735	FAX: 225-9580

SOUTH CAROLINA

Senators:

Strom Thurmond	OFFICE: 224-5972	FAX: 224-1300
Ernest F. Hollings	OFFICE: 224-6121	FAX: 224-3573

Representatives:

1st	Arthur Ravenel, Jr.	OFFICE: 225-3176	FAX: 225-4340
2nd	Floyd Spence	OFFICE: 225-2452	FAX: 225-2455
3rd	Butler Derrick	OFFICE: 225-5301	FAX: unavailable
4th	Elizabeth J. Patterson	OFFICE: 225-6030	FAX: 225-7664
5th	John M. Spratt, Jr.	OFFICE: 225-5501	FAX: 225-0464
6th	Robin M. Tallon	OFFICE: 225-3315	FAX: 225-2857

SOUTH DAKOTA

Senators:

Larry Pressler	OFFICE: 224-5842	FAX: unavailable
Thomas A. Daschle	OFFICE: 224-2321	FAX: 224-2047

Representative:

Tim Johnson	OFFICE: 225-2801	FAX: 225-2427

TENNESSEE

Senators:

James Sasser	OFFICE: 224-3344	FAX: 224-9590
Albert Gore, Jr	OFFICE: 224-4944	FAX: unavailable

Representatives:

1st	James H. Quillen	OFFICE: 225-6356	FAX: 225-7812
2nd	John J. Duncan, Jr.	OFFICE: 225-5435	FAX: 225-6440
3rd	Marilyn Lloyd	OFFICE: 225-3271	FAX: 225-6974
4th	Jim Cooper	OFFICE: 225-6831	FAX: 225-4520
5th	Bob Clement	OFFICE: 225-4311	FAX: 226-1035
6th	Bart Gordon	OFFICE: 225-4231	FAX: 225-6887
7th	Don Sundquist	OFFICE: 225-2811	FAX: 225-2814
8th	John S. Tanner	OFFICE: 225-4714	FAX: 225-1765

9th   Harold E. Ford   OFFICE: 225-3265   FAX: 225-9215

TEXAS

Senators:

Lloyd Bentsen   OFFICE: 224-5922   FAX: unavailable
Phil Gramm   OFFICE: 224-2934   FAX: unavailable

Representatives:

1st	Jim Chapman	OFFICE: 225-3035	FAX: 225-7265
2nd	Charles Wilson	OFFICE: 225-2401	FAX: 225-1764
3rd	Steve Bartlett	OFFICE: 225-4201	FAX: unavailable
4th	Ralph M. Hall	OFFICE: 225-6673	FAX: 225-3332
5th	John Bryant	OFFICE: 225-2231	FAX: 225-9721
6th	Joe L. Barton	OFFICE: 225-2002	FAX: 225-3052
7th	Bill Archer	OFFICE: 225-2571	FAX: 225-4381
8th	Jack Fields	OFFICE: 225-4901	FAX: 225-6899
9th	Jack Brooks	OFFICE: 225-6565	FAX: 225-1584
10th	J.J. Pickler	OFFICE: 225-4865	FAX: unavailable
11th	Marvin Leath	OFFICE: 225-6105	FAX: 225-0350
12th	Pete Geren	OFFICE: 225-5071	FAX: unavailable
13th	Bill Sarpalius	OFFICE: 225-3706	FAX: 225-6142
14th	Greg Laughlin	OFFICE: 225-2831	FAX: unavailable
15th	E. de la (Kika) Garza	OFFICE: 225-2531	FAX: 225-2533
16th	Ronald D. Coleman	OFFICE: 225-4831	FAX: unavailable
17th	Charles W. Stenholm	OFFICE: 225-6605	FAX: 225-2234
18th	Mickey Leland	OFFICE: 225-3816	FAX: unavailable
19th	Larry Combest	OFFICE: 225-4005	FAX: 225-9615
20th	Henry B. Gonzalez	OFFICE: 225-3236	FAX: 225-1915
21st	Lamar S. Smith	OFFICE: 225-4236	FAX: 225-8628
22nd	Tom DeLay	OFFICE: 225-5951	FAX: 225-4251
23rd	Albert G. Bustamante	OFFICE: 225-4511	FAX: unavailalbe
24th	Martin Frost	OFFICE: 225-3605	FAX: 225-4951
25th	Michael A. Andrews	OFFICE: 225-7508	FAX: 225-4210
26th	Richard K. Armey	OFFICE: 225-7772	FAX: 225-7614
27th	Soloman P. Ortiz	OFFICE: 225-7742	FAX: 226-1134

UTAH

Senators:

Jake Garn	OFFICE: 224-5444	FAX: unavailable
Orrin G. Hatch	OFFICE: 224-5251	FAX: 224-6331

Representatives:

1st	James V. Hansen	OFFICE: 225-0453	FAX: 225-5857
2nd	Wayne Owens	OFFICE: 225-3011	FAX: 225-3524
3rd	Howard C. Nielson	OFFICE: 225-7751	FAX: 226-1223

VERMONT

Senators:

James M. Jeffords	OFFICE: 224-5141	FAX: 224-1507
Patrick J. Leahy	OFFICE: 224-4242	FAX: 224-4797

Representatives:

Peter Smith	OFFICE: 225-4115	FAX: 225-6790

VIRGINIA

Senators:

John William Warner	OFFICE: 224-2023	FAX: 224-6295
Charles S. Robb	OFFICE: 224-4024	FAX: 224-8689

Representatives:

1st	Herbert H. Bateman	OFFICE: 225-4261	FAX: 225-4382
2nd	Owen B. Pickett	OFFICE: 225-4215	FAX: 225-4218
3rd	Thomas J. Bliley, Jr.	OFFICE: 225-2815	FAX: none listed
4th	Norman Sisisky	OFFICE: 225-6365	FAX: 225-1469
5th	Lewis F. Payne, Jr.	OFFICE: 225-4771	FAX: 226-1147
6th	James Olin	OFFICE: 225-5431	FAX: 225-9623
7th	D. French Slaughter, Jr.	OFFICE: 225-6561	FAX: 225-0500
8th	Stan Parris	OFFICE: 225-4376	FAX: 225-0017
9th	Rick Boucher	OFFICE: 225-3861	FAX: unavailable
10th	Frank R. Wolf	OFFICE: 225-5136	FAX: 225-0437

WASHINGTON

Senators:

Slade Gorton	OFFICE: 224-3441	FAX: 224-9393
Brock Adams	OFFICE: 224-2621	FAX: 224-0238

Representatives:

1st	John Miller	OFFICE: 225-6311	FAX: unavailable
2nd	Al Swift	OFFICE: 225-2605	FAX: unavailable
3rd	Jolene Unsoeld	OFFICE: 225-3536	FAX: 225-9095
4th	Sid Morrison	OFFICE: 225-5816	FAX: 225-9293
5th	Thomas S. Foley	OFFICE: 225-2006	FAX: unavailable
6th	Norman D. Dicks	OFFICE: 225-5916	FAX: 226-1176
7th	Jim McDermott	OFFICE: 225-3106	FAX: unavailable
8th	Rod Chandler	OFFICE: 225-7761	FAX: 225-0035

WEST VIRGINIA

Senators:

Robert C. Byrd	OFFICE: 224-3954	FAX: 224-8070
John D. (Jay) Rockefeller, IV	OFFICE: 224-6472	FAX: 224-1689

Representatives:

1st	Alan B. Mollohan	OFFICE: 225-4172	FAX: 225-7564
2nd	Harley O. Staggers, Jr.	OFFICE: 225-4331	FAX: 225-2962
3rd	Robert E. Wise Jr.	OFFICE: 225-2711	FAX: 225-5325
4th	Nick Joe Rahall, II	OFFICE: 225-3452	FAX: unavailable

WISCONSIN

Senators:

Herbert H. Kohl	OFFICE: 224-5653	FAX: 224-9787
Robert W. Kasten, Jr.	OFFICE: 224-5323	FAX: 224-2548

Representatives:

1st	Les Aspin	OFFICE: 225-3031	FAX: unavailable
2nd	Robert W. Kastenmeier	OFFICE: 225-2906	FAX: unavailable
3rd	Steve Gunderson	OFFICE: 225-5506	FAX: 225-6195

4th	Gerald D. Kleczka	OFFICE: 225-4572	FAX: 225-0719
5th	Jim Moody	OFFICE: 225-3571	FAX: 225-1396
6th	Thomas E. Petri	OFFICE: 225-2476	FAX: unavailable
7th	David R. Obey	OFFICE: 225-3365	FAX: 225-0561
8th	Toby Roth	OFFICE: 225-5665	FAX: 225-0087
9th	F. James Sensenbrenner, Jr.	OFFICE: 225-5101	FAX: 225-3190

WYOMING

Senators:

| Malcolm Wallop | OFFICE: 224-6441 | FAX: 224-3230 |
| Alan K. Simpson | OFFICE: 224-3424 | FAX: 224-1315 |

Representative:

| Craig Thomas | OFFICE: 225-2311 | FAX: unavailable |

About the Author

Mark Harris is a writer who lives in Chicago. He hopes that *Embracing the Earth* will inspire others to become involved in improving their own communities and to join in a worldwide effort to care for our earth.